The Mujahedin-e Khalq (MEK)
Shackled by a Twisted History

COMMENTS ON THIS REPORT

I thoroughly appreciated Linc Bloomfield's thoughtful debunking of the many myths surrounding the Mujahedin-e Khalq (MEK). During my time as the Commander in Iraq from 2004–2007, my intelligence analysts struggled to reconcile reports about the MEK's past with reports from our leaders at Camp Ashraf on their daily interactions with the MEK. We would have welcomed this detailed look at their history. Now that the MEK has been removed from the list of Foreign Terrorist Organizations, this insightful piece paves the way for an open discussion of their potential future role.

>   **General George W. Casey, Jr., USA (Ret.)**
>   36th Chief of Staff, United States Army, and
>   former Commanding General,
>   Multi-National Force-Iraq

Linc Bloomfield, a proven State Department veteran, shreds the US Government's flawed understanding of the MEK, both current and historic; he debunks previously-believed studies and bureaucratically-perpetuated myths, and finally presents an unbiased review of the MEK's history and goals. This is long overdue, and a serious read for national security leaders developing regional and international policy on the MEK after its de-listing. It is time to dump the "old think" of skeptics viewing the MEK as unsavory and cult-like, and let the MEK successfully rehabilitate itself. We should welcome the MEK as a counter balance to Tehran and an intelligence resource against that hated regime, and recognize that its campaign for a regime change offers hope for a future Iran committed to forgoing nuclear weapons and joining the community of responsible nations.

>   **Lieutenant General Dell L. Dailey, USA (Ret.)**
>   former Coordinator for Counterterrorism and
>   Ambassador at Large, US Department of State, and
>   Director, Center for Special Operations,
>   US Special Operations Command

Ambassador Bloomfield has done everyone who has been involved with the issue of the MEK/NCRI issue a great service. Based on my brief association with the plight of the refugees of Camp Ashraf, and given the brutal behavior of Iraqi forces towards people who voluntarily surrendered their arms to US authorities in 2003, Ambassador Bloomfield's objective and thorough review of the history of the relationship since the early 1970s is a study that needs to be read by all. His work will be particularly useful to those in our administration charged with developing policy that is fair and consistent with the facts, to those in the media who have been overly closed-minded on the issue, and to those Members of Congress who have fought valiantly to do the right thing. As is always true when dealing with complex situations, truth is often obscured by unfounded rhetoric. Ambassador Bloomfield's work zeroes in on explaining the truth about this piece of history.

>   **General James L. Jones, USMC (Ret.)**
>   former U.S. National Security Advisor,
>   Supreme Allied Commander, NATO and
>   Commander, US European Command, and
>   32nd Commandant, United States Marine Corps

Ambassador Lincoln P. Bloomfield Jr. has written an exhaustively researched and un-blinking study of how and why the Iranian organization known as Mujahedin-e Khalq (MEK), fervently opposed to the theocracy that governs that country, came to be designated unjustifiably by our State Department as a foreign terrorist organization, and how some within that agency continue to obstruct any attempt to correct the record even after that designation has been removed. Painstakingly, he shows the falsity of various accusations that MEK members participated in violence, analyzes how those accusations might have arisen in view of MEK's opposition to the Shah before the 1979 revolution, and then shows that particular false accusations were first presented in State Department country analyses, then removed, but then reinserted even in the absence of new evidence when policy considerations made it convenient to do so. This study portrays—devastatingly—how bureaucratic commitment to a point of view eventually can drive some within that bureaucracy to fight the impingement of inconvenient reality on their policy-driven view of the world.

Judge Michael B. Mukasey
81st Attorney General of the United States, and
former Judge and Chief Judge, United States District Court for
the Southern District of New York

Through meticulous analysis and a sophisticated understanding of the actors and politics of the Middle East, Ambassador Bloomfield has deconstructed and demystified the allegations, misunderstandings and disinformation surrounding the MEK. His analysis provides the most accurate assessment publicly available for understanding this long-maligned organization, placing it in its proper local and historical context in pre- and post-revolutionary Iran. Bloomfield's research not only provides important answers about the MEK, it also raises significant questions about the objectivity and competence of State Department officials.

Hon. Mitchell B. Reiss
27th President of Washington College, and
former Director of Policy Planning and
Ambassador/Special Envoy, US Department of State

In unveiling the State Department's first Quadrennial Diplomacy and Development Review, Secretary Clinton asked, "How can we do better?" A good start would be to study this report and determine how an important US policy became so utterly disconnected from the facts over many years. Ambassador Linc Bloomfield's account is tough but fair in setting the record straight. As someone who has held senior policy positions at State, he holds the government to account for its many shortcomings on this issue but without denigrating those who serve. This report will benefit the policy process in Washington as the US seeks more effective approaches to avoiding a nuclear-armed Iran.

Governor Bill Richardson
30th Governor of New Mexico, and
former Secretary of Energy, US Ambassador /
Permanent Representative to the United Nations,
and Member of Congress

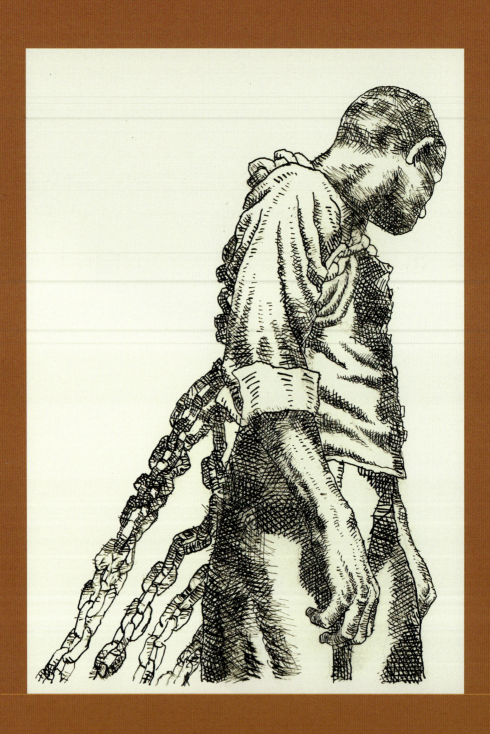

The Mujahedin-e Khalq (MEK)
Shackled by a Twisted History

by Lincoln P. Bloomfield, Jr.

College of Public Affairs

Copyright © 2013
University of Baltimore
College of Public Affairs
1420 N. Charles St.
Baltimore, MD 21201-5779
www.ubalt.edu

All rights reserved. No part of this publication may be reproduced or transmitted in any form or by any means, electronic or mechanical, including photocopy, recording or any information storage and retrieval system, without permission in writing from the publisher.

Printed in the United States of America.
First edition.
ISBN 978-0-615-78384

Library of Congress Control Number: 2013935610

Cover and frontispiece illustration of enchained humanity by Brad Holland. Book design by the Office of University Relations at the University of Baltimore and by Auburn Associates, Inc.

ACKNOWLEDGMENTS

The author is grateful to the University of Baltimore, in particular Provost Joseph Wood and Dean Stephen Percy, for their support in bringing this work to the public domain. Vice President for Planning and External Affairs, Peter Toran, Director of University Relations, Gabrielle "Gigi" Boam, and Senior Graphic Designer, James "JJ" Chrystal led a team of talented professionals at the University who produced this publication from a simple manuscript. I am honored that renowned artist Brad Holland graced the project by creating the cover and frontispiece illustration. I thank Generals Jones, Casey and Dailey, Judge Mukasey, Dr. Reiss and Governor Richardson, each among the most accomplished and respected public servants of our time, for reviewing this study and providing their comments.

The lion's share of my gratitude, however, is reserved for Dr. Ivan Sascha Sheehan, Director of the graduate programs in Negotiation and Conflict Management and Global Affairs and Human Security in the School of Public and International Affairs. Professor Sheehan's skill in mobilizing the necessary participants and shepherding this project to completion with remarkable tact, speed, and precision was an inspiration, surpassed only by his eloquence in framing the study with the Foreword essay that follows.

To the extent that this monograph reflects genuine understanding of the MEK, the author is indebted to members and supporters of the organization for continuously making themselves available over the past two years, patiently answering countless queries, and responding constructively to the author's efforts to probe and verify points of information. The attempt has been made throughout to present what I judge to be the truth in depicting issues and events, using the most credible information available and identifying both pro- and anti-MEK sources where a question of bias may be relevant. As ever, I stand ready to be corrected should any point of fact or analysis be contradicted by superior evidence.

Notwithstanding the extensive effort by others that made this publication possible, responsibility for any errors that may be found herein is mine alone. My modest hope is that the reader will find within these pages an impetus to ask important questions and search anew for satisfactory answers. Should this body of work lead colleagues, in the US or abroad, in the public or private sectors, to evaluate the MEK and its history with a fresh perspective, I believe that the public interest will have been served.

Lincoln P. Bloomfield, Jr.
Alexandria, Virginia
March 6, 2013

"To those new States whom we welcome to the ranks of the free, we pledge our word that one form of colonial control shall not have passed away merely to be replaced by a far more iron tyranny. We shall not always expect to find them supporting our view. But we shall always hope to find them strongly supporting their own freedom ...."

—President John F. Kennedy
Inaugural Address, January 20, 1961

FOREWORD

by Dr. Ivan Sascha Sheehan

History is replete with figures that have failed to bridge life in the public forum and life in the ivory tower. Public officials whose political pronouncements are not supported by available evidence are common. So too are scholars who, to avoid controversy, only study matters for which there is little utility and sometimes no immediate application.

In the pages that follow, Ambassador Lincoln P. Bloomfield, Jr., a public servant who has served three US presidents in five administrations and operated at senior levels of government over the past thirty-two years, suffers from no such conflict as he challenges Washington's conventional thinking on US-Iran policy.

In this groundbreaking study, Bloomfield brings his sterling reputation, attention for detail, and knowledge of US Government policymaking to bear on the most pressing security concern of our time: the management of an increasingly belligerent, nearly nuclear-armed Iran and the treatment of the Islamic Republic's best organized and most determined grassroots opposition.

The author draws on extensive experience as a senior foreign policy and defense official to craft a careful, scholarly narrative that outlines how the actual history of the Mujahedin-e Khalq (MEK)—a group that was formed to oppose the Shah but fell out with the regime of Ayatollah Khomeini—came to be "twisted" for diplomatic ends. He shows how US officials found it expedient to view political conflict as terrorism to promote a policy of engagement with Tehran and identifies the contemporary implications of these decisions for US foreign policy.

Bloomfield is admittedly hard on the State Department but, as a former Special Envoy and Assistant Secretary of State, he is also sensitive to the difficult tasks carried out by senior government officials. His intent is not simply to criticize but to correct misperceptions and errors of fact—many secretly promoted in foreign capitals by Iranian security services—that led to MEK's terror tagging in the first place and persuaded administrations of both parties to sustain it. In so doing, he sets the stage for a fresh evaluation of Iran's primary opposition to clerical rule.

Bloomfield's report is the most comprehensive and compelling rebuttal to the US Government file on MEK to date and it is certain to shift Washington's view on the nature and history of Iran's political resistance.

Seldom do authors so eloquently challenge conventional thinking, correct the public record, and combine academic rigor with sound policy recommendations. Bloomfield proves that it is possible to be contemplative without falling victim to moral equivalency and that constraints on leadership do not provide immunity from accountability for policy missteps that have national security and human rights dimensions.

Washington's Clinton-era decision to succumb to Iranian demands to contain their opposition was intended to secure Tehran's compliance with international norms. It backfired. The decades-long struggle to please Tehran through negotiations and open-ended discussions only telegraphed weakness. Political engagement did not stem the tide of proxy violence nor did appeasement provide the impetus for Iran's theocrats to join the civilized world. Instead, a willingness to negotiate over the opposition's fate proved a weak negotiating posture and denied the world access to a key ally in containing Iranian aggression. Listing the MEK as a terrorist group was to become a bipartisan failure as successive US presidents bowed to Iranian demands in an effort to capitulate and concede their way toward a more peaceful relationship.

US Secretary of State Hillary Clinton's September 2012 decision to remove the organization's terror designation was the shot heard around the world. The MEK's removal from the State Department's Foreign Terrorist Organization list was an acknowledgement that the group failed to meet the statutory criteria necessary for the designation. The US Court of Appeals issuance of a deadline by which the Secretary had to remove the listing or face judicial oversight was further incentive to act. But the move was also an illustration of the growing bipartisan consensus that the group's resistance represented a useful political check on the regime's regional influence and the best hope for a more peaceful and stable Iran. That the MEK had been a valuable and consistent source of intelligence on Iran's emerging nuclear weapons program was further indication of the group's constructive intent.

Some heralded Ms. Clinton's decision as the clearest indication to date that the policy of unending diplomatic engagement with the Iranian regime was over. Others took that all options for Iran's containment—including preemptive strikes—would be open for consideration.

A commentary I co-authored titled *Now the Cards are on the Table*, published in Israel's *Haaretz* on the morning of the State Department delisting announcement, concluded that Secretary Clinton's decision to remove the group's terror label marked an opportunity to reset Iran policy by embracing regime change from within as a priority and adopting a fresh approach toward the Iranian opposition.

On the heels of Ms. Clinton's decision and global calls for a new policy toward the MEK, Bloomfield's report takes on Washington's misconceptions by exposing and deconstructing Washington's policy initiatives and MEK myths in a manner that is at once informative, lively, readable, and well documented but also critical and, at times, even scathing.

On reading his report, I was reminded of Hans Christian Andersen's fable of two weavers who swindle a vain emperor into buying a suit of clothes that is invisible to those who are unfit or stupid. Unable to see his own outfit but determined not to let anybody know lest they think *he* is stupid, he proceeds to the public square where he is met by others who, hearing of the emperor's magical clothes, also fear appearing stupid and congratulate him on his attire. It is left to a child to point out the obvious: "but the emperor is not wearing any clothes!" One can't help wondering how many Washington insiders willingly shared in perpetuating the poisonous image and allegations attached to the MEK—despite what we now know was a wealth of available evidence to the contrary—and were thus complicit in the suppression and mistreatment of Iran's opposition.

I first met Ambassador Bloomfield in the spring of 2012 when we appeared on a panel together at George Mason University alongside Professor Alan Dershowitz of Harvard Law School and former US Attorney General Michael Mukasey. The panel addressed US policy toward Iran in the context of the multilateral nuclear negotiations designed to curtail Iran's enrichment of uranium to weapons grade levels. Among the issues discussed at the event were the Iranian regime's deplorable human rights record, its longstanding campaign of state-sponsored proxy violence, and the options available to US policymakers seeking to promote peaceful, democratic change in Tehran.

I later met with Bloomfield in Paris where we were separately studying the Iranian resistance, meeting with exiles, and examining public statements and documents issued by resistance figures—including President-Elect Maryam Rajavi, the leader of the National Council of Resistance of Iran (NCRI). The NCRI, a Paris-based coalition of opposition organizations that reject clerical rule and stand for democratic change, serves as the opposition's parliament in exile and is widely regarded as the democratic alternative to the Ayatollahs.

During these meetings I was struck by Bloomfield's detailed understanding of the challenges posed by Iran and the careful manner with which he assessed the actions of policymakers and the evolution of US policy after the 1979 Revolution.

At a private dinner following a resistance rally in Paris, Bloomfield and I both heard a former UN human rights official in Iraq tell of his resignation from the mission and the direct role being exercised by Iran, but concealed from UN headquarters in New York, in the movement of Iranian exiles from Camp Ashraf to Camp Liberty. Ambassador Bloomfield subsequently arranged to bring the official to Washington and ensured that his important revelations were made known to senior officials and members of Congress.

At a moment when public officials are often captive to preconceived ideological inclinations and talking points featuring thin analyses, Bloomfield's prescriptions for addressing the Iran threat are sensible, grounded in evidence, and certain to have an impact across the political spectrum.

That national leadership figures as respected and distinguished as General James Jones, General George Casey, Lieutenant General Dell Dailey, Judge Michael Mukasey, Dr. Mitchell

Reiss, and Governor Bill Richardson would provide support and encouragement for the findings in this report speaks to its importance. Such endorsements are also indicative of Ambassador Bloomfield's reputation as a policy practitioner and expert in international affairs.

This publication arrives at a decisive moment when Iran's clerical rulers are on increasingly shaky ground. Ordinary Iranians are angry and restless. With their currency in free fall and an economy hampered by sanctions imposed by the international community to prevent Iran's rise as a nuclear power, the regime's leaders are looking to shift attention from domestic troubles by suppressing dissent, silencing minority voices, and pledging solidarity with the world's tyrants.

Iran's vast petroleum exports have so far shielded the regime from outright collapse but enhanced sanctions are taking a toll and a financial crisis looms large. With prices rising, inflation threatens social cohesion and discontent on the Iranian street is certain to continue its rise. To distract from its mounting internal woes, the regime has dug in by closing ranks with Shi'ite officials in Baghdad, expanding their violent arc of influence to include Damascus, Lebanon, Gaza, and the Arabian Gulf, and engaging in escalating rhetoric with the US and Israel while defying international nuclear norms.

If past is prologue, the regime is also likely to lash out at its most feared resistance. The regime has long sought to break the back of the MEK's organized opposition through harassment and violence. Attacks in 2009 and 2011 left scores injured and killed. In 2012, three-thousand vulnerable dissidents were transferred from Camp Ashraf, their home for decades, to a so-called temporary transfer facility run by the Maliki government in Iraq that is alternately described as deplorable and in utter disrepair.

On February 9, 2013, Camp Liberty came under missile and mortar attack during the early dawn hours by "unknown assailants." Seven individuals, including a woman, were killed in the attack and more than fifty were injured. In the weeks following the slaughter, three additional individuals died while being denied adequate medical treatment in Iraq. The attack likely originated with orders from the Islamic Republic's Supreme Leader, Ayatollah Ali Khamenei, and was facilitated by the Quds Force, a paramilitary wing of the Iranian Revolutionary Guards Corps, with assistance from the Shi'ite government in Iraq.

In spite of these setbacks, the MEK maintains a vast and intricate network of global support and a capacity to organize so sophisticated as to rival that of any political party the world over. The realization that there is a viable political alternative in the Iranian opposition has only increased calls for democratic change in Tehran. A bipartisan chorus of leading figures in the US Congress, and parliamentarians from around the world, are now expressing their belief that Iranians should be able to choose their leaders in free and fair elections without fear of intimidation or reprisal and that the time has come for real change in Tehran.

A previous study of the MEK concluded that its stated positions and goals over many years had been consistent with democratic principles. The world will next need to consider whether a non-nuclear Iran that strives for human rights, gender equality, separation of church and state, freedom of speech, and positive relations with global powers is best achieved through a preemptive military campaign or through more robust and effective non-military support of those seeking regime change from within.

As the regime continues to deny the Iranian people an opportunity make their voices heard by tightly controlling participation in elections, Ambassador Bloomfield's report is a wake-up call for US officials who have fallen victim to misinformation and a guide for those seeking fresh policy prescriptions. The study is also a reality check on the regime's well-coordinated propaganda campaign and a reminder to those on the Iranian street—and their many supporters worldwide—that, while political change takes time, the arc of history bends towards justice.

Ivan Sascha Sheehan, Ph.D.
Assistant Professor and Director,
Negotiation and Conflict Management Program &
Global Affairs and Human Security Program
School of Public and International Affairs
College of Public Affairs
University of Baltimore

The Mujahedin-e Khalq (MEK)
Shackled by a Twisted History

by Lincoln P. Bloomfield, Jr.

"When you develop your opinions on the basis of weak evidence, you will have difficulty interpreting subsequent information that contradicts your opinions, even if this new information is obviously more accurate."

Nassim Nicholas Taleb,
The Black Swan

Introduction

As much as the American public lionizes the military for the terrible burdens it is asked to bear, the Department of State is also sometimes handed thankless tasks in untenable circumstances, with important interests at stake. Such has been the case over the past year with State's effort to manage the relocation and future disposition of 3,200 Iranian expatriates inside Iraq, while responding to a US federal Appeals Court challenge by their organizational affiliate known as the Mujahedin-e Khalq, or MEK, seeking the lifting of its 15-year-long US designation as a Foreign Terrorist Organization (FTO).

Secretary of State Hillary Clinton surprised a lot of veteran foreign policy observers in September 2012 by deciding to revoke the MEK's FTO designation just days before the US Court of Appeals for the District of Columbia Circuit was planning to do the same. In doing so she averted the worst scenario under the 1996 law (as amended in 2004) governing terrorism listings—the perception that the court had removed a foreign organization on legal procedural grounds while the executive branch continued to regard it as a terrorist threat to US interests. The MEK, the September 28, 2012 announcement made clear, was de-listed because of *"the absence of confirmed acts of terrorism by the MEK for more than a decade …."*

The MEK had long pressured the State Department to lift the terrorist designation, dating back to 1997 when it was first listed as a Foreign Terrorist Organization. And yet, through Republican and Democratic administrations, claims by the MEK that its past activities and true nature had been misstated and misunderstood failed to persuade Washington to change its view. Over the past two years, a large and growing list of American notables, including former Governors, Cabinet secretaries and senior military officers, has advocated forcefully on behalf of the MEK, most calling for decisive action to assure the safety of the exiles inside Iraq as well as the de-listing of the MEK as a FTO. Congressional sympathizers in both parties have similarly pressed the MEK's case with the Administration, with the House in 2009 fielding 224 co-sponsors on a resolution supportive of the MEK. Many of these legislators and ex-officials have embraced the Paris-based National Council of Resistance of Iran (NCRI), the political organization of which the MEK is the main component, as a counterweight to the Tehran government and its threatening behavior.

Despite its being de-listed, no one in the US foreign policy community including officials, think tank analysts or journalists appears to doubt that, as their reports and commentaries have unfailingly reiterated, the MEK has a grim history of terrorism, including killing Americans, attacking US properties, and supporting the 1979 Embassy hostage-taking. Reports in recent years from respected institutions including the RAND Corporation and Human Rights Watch have reinforced a dark portrayal of the MEK that, on a human and ideological as well as policy level, cannot but invite contempt and lasting aversion.

What support this exiled resistance group has received on Capitol Hill and from ex-officials has been disparaged by some as an unwise application of the adage 'the enemy of my enemy is my friend.' A generation of policy officials has dealt with MEK representatives and is familiar with its claims to have been maligned in official, academic and media descriptions; still, inside the Washington Beltway the MEK is widely presumed guilty of serious transgressions.

With such a heavy dossier repeatedly validated over many years by Administrations of both parties despite its unceasing efforts to revisit US policy, the MEK's sudden delisting by the Secretary of State appeared to many to be a tactical expedient, a tolerable concession in support of a larger goal. Both Iraq and Iran had demanded the closure of Camp Ashraf northeast of Baghdad, home to as many as 3,800 MEK members since 1986 and its primary base of operations against the Iranian regime. In February 2012, Secretary Clinton had publicly linked the possibility of de-listing to the MEK's cooperation in relocating from

Camp Ashraf to a site in Baghdad formerly known to US forces as Camp Liberty, for processing by the United Nations as potential refugees.

Once all MEK personnel but a small close-out team had departed from Camp Ashraf, the decision lifting the designation was issued. Mrs. Clinton's stature undoubtedly muted criticism of her decision, yet many news stories portrayed it as misguided, with damning and pejorative descriptions of the MEK and quotes from policy officials cautioning against any US steps that would promote the activities of such a group.

For officials, journalists and experts alike, the willingness of so many former national leaders—including a US Attorney General, an FBI Director, a Secretary of Homeland Security, a National Security Advisor, a Homeland Security Advisor, a Speaker of the House of Representatives, a State Department Counterterrorism Coordinator, two CIA Directors, three military service Chiefs, four governors and three Chairmen of the Joint Chiefs of Staff, among many other general officers, ambassadors and subcabinet officials—to have advocated precisely such a reversal of policy could be explained only by their receipt of monetary compensation.

And so, the conventional wisdom in Washington today holds that the MEK remains dangerous—a coercive cult with American blood on its hands, whose latter-day professions of democratic leanings mask a longstanding radical, anti-American and dictatorial bent. Removal of the MEK from the terrorism list is understood, if at all, as a simple acknowledgement that the group has refrained from terror operations in recent years—nothing more. So long as the US Government takes no additional steps to advantage the MEK as an organization, Secretary Clinton will get credit for having managed the exiles' relocation from Camp Ashraf about as well as could be expected amid distractions and pressures from all sides.

There is, however, one problem with this policy consensus on the MEK: the facts support the prevailing wisdom far less, and the MEK's claims far more, than the US Government, the media and the foreign policy community would likely believe possible.

A large part of what credentialed authorities have been saying in the US about the MEK's past is—whether they realize it or not—either demonstrably untrue, factually unsupportable or misleading to the point of intellectual dishonesty. What remains after filtering out the false and distorted aspects of the MEK's history has been judged by British and French judicial authorities as constituting legitimate armed resistance to tyranny, and not as activity meeting accepted definitions of terrorism. Alleged past MEK misdeeds against the United States are, in the same vein, recounted today in verbal formulations so untethered to the actual history as to misassign responsibility for these terrible acts which Washington still understandably regards as unforgivable.

This review of the MEK's history attempts to measure widespread beliefs and perceptions—particularly within Washington DC policy circles—regarding the MEK's actions and nature over the group's 47-year existence against the factual record. Information sources supporting the author's analysis are identified throughout. The reader will see that both the disturbing image and condemnable record of activities by the MEK assumed to be accurate by most in the press, the public and US Government agencies cannot be reconciled with the evidence. This history has been 'twisted,' and in several key respects the facts wholly undermine the conclusions many have drawn about the MEK, with profound consequences.

A discrepancy of such magnitude between American perception and reality, the product of many factors, is not entirely accidental. To examine, clarify and correct the MEK's record is to encounter an array of revealed strategic liabilities, begging the question of what costs these could exact on US interests going forward.

Trusted Sources, Corrupted

On July 16, 2010, the federal Appeals Court, ruling on Department of State documents submitted in August, September and October of the previous year, said "[W]e are unsure what material the Secretary in fact relied on or to what portion of [the legal criteria for listing a FTO] she found it relevant."[1] Secretary Clinton was at a disadvantage, being asked to justify a decision to maintain the MEK designation made by her predecessor, Secretary Condoleezza Rice, days before leaving office in January 2009. The Court instructed Secretary Clinton to go back and "indicate in her administrative summary which sources she regards as sufficiently credible that she relies upon them …." More than two years later—no such sources having been produced in court—the Secretary de-listed the MEK.

In the absence of a court submission from the executive branch, the public's sole official resource for facts about the MEK is the Department of State's *Country Reports on Terrorism*, issued annually by the Bureau of Counterterrorism. In the wake of years of intense judicial scrutiny and the post-9/11 Global War on Terrorism, one would expect to find the *Country Reports* section on the MEK meticulously researched, a paragon of historical precision. Instead, the 2011 report, issued on July 31, 2012, is studded with assertions that raise alarming concerns about the US Government's grasp of the facts. Consider:

The NLA. The 2011 report begins by describing the MEK as *"a Marxist-Islamic Organization that seeks the overthrow of the Iranian regime through its military wing, the National Liberation Army (NLA), and its political front, the National Council of Resistance of Iran (NCRI)."*

The NLA has been out of existence for over nine years. It had already ceased to exist four years before this error first appeared in the 2007 *Country Reports*, yet it has been repeated annually ever since. The MEK's military capability ended in 2003 when the MEK in Iraq disarmed and turned its weapons over to the US Army 4th Infantry Division. While the 2011 *Country Reports* says the MEK gave up its *"heavy-arms"* to Coalition forces, in fact the 4th ID commander, Major General Raymond Odierno (now US Army Chief of Staff) briefed the press at the time on the precise inventory of weapons collected, including an estimated 10,000 small arms, stating, *"We have taken all small arms…."*[2]

As former US military officers responsible for security at Camp Ashraf have pointed out, the MEK well understood from 2003 on that the discovery of even a single weapon at Camp Ashraf would have triggered far more intrusive and restrictive Rules of Engagement for the US forces guarding them. When Iraqi military forces entered Camp Ashraf and attacked the residents in July 2009 and again in April 2011, killing 49 and wounding several hundred, the population was defenseless and, as the UN officer on the scene recounted, *"not a single Iraqi soldier was even scratched."*[3]

Terrorists? The 2011 report says *"The group's worldwide campaign against the Iranian government uses propaganda and terrorism to achieve its objectives."*

This allegation is, of course, superseded by the September 2012 de-listing. The Appeals Court brief of July 16, 2010 cited the MEK's petition arguing that more than a decade earlier, in 2001, it had ceased military operations against the Iranian regime, disbanded military units and renounced violence, and had turned over its weapons to US forces in Iraq in 2003. US military officers responsible for Camp Ashraf and surrounding areas during Operation Iraqi Freedom (OIF) have testified to Congress that in 2003 and 2004 every person at Camp Ashraf was investigated by US intelligence and law enforcement officials and none was found to have been a combatant or broken any US laws. In 2004 each one signed a document negotiated with the US rejecting violence and terror.

Court challenges in the UK and EU in recent years resulted in rulings that the MEK was not engaged in or planning terrorist activities, and the group was also removed from those terrorism lists. As explained in the next item below, a French terror prosecution reached the same result. The author's August 2011 review of public domain information yielded no substantiated evidence of any such activities by the MEK over the past decade.[4] Nevertheless, there was one event within the last decade deemed worthy of inclusion in the *Country Reports*:

The 2003 Paris Headquarters Raid.
The 2011 report says, *"In 2003, French authorities arrested 160 MEK members at operational bases they believed the MEK was using to coordinate financing and planning for terrorist attacks. ... French authorities eventually released [Maryam] Rajavi."*

Some US officials may still believe the French authorities were on a bona fide counterterrorism mission that day, but the rest of the world knows otherwise, thanks to a respected journalist's first-hand account which revealed the true story in scandalous detail. Jean-Claude Maurice, former senior reporter and later editor of the *Journal du Dimanche,* accompanied then-French Foreign Minister Dominique de Villepin on a visit to Iran in 2003.

As chronicled in his 2009 memoir, *Si vous le répétez, je démentirai...Chirac, Sarkozy, Villepin* ("If you repeat it, I will deny it"), after the press was dismissed at the outset of Minister Villepin's meeting with Iran's Foreign Minister Kamal Kharrazi, Mr. Maurice ducked back

Figure 1.
Former French Foreign Minister Dominique de Villepin being satirized. Courtesy Iran National TV.

into the meeting room to retrieve his briefcase but was kept from exiting and told to sit as guards closed the doors. The Ministers did not know of his presence. His summary of the conversation had Mr. Villepin promoting *Total's* interest in securing a major Iranian oil concession by offering a state visit to Iran by President Chirac. The nuclear issue and human rights were also discussed.

Rising at the end to see his guest off, Foreign Minister Kharrazi explicitly requested, as a "deliverable" from France, that France take action against the MEK. Kharrazi said that Iran's Ambassador to France was standing by to coordinate with then-Interior Minister Nicolas Sarkozy. Shortly thereafter, French authorities staged a spectacular raid on the NCRI involving 1,300 police officers, arresting Mrs. Maryam Rajavi and 159 others in their homes. MEK exiles in France panicked, fearing they would be shipped back to Iran to face incarceration and probable execution. *Total* was awarded a significant oil concession by Iran.

At the conclusion of a thorough judicial process, in April 2011, the French Investigative Magistrate dismissed all charges against the NCRI with these words: *"The dossier does not contain any evidence indicating an armed activity that would intentionally target civilians. If such evidence were available it would confirm terrorism and would annul any reference to resistance against tyranny ...."*

Today, the episode is fodder for humorous videos caricaturing the French and Iranian officials involved in the scheme, produced in Europe and broadcast via satellite into Iran and beyond (Figure 1).

The Mujahedin-e Khalq (MEK)

Until Secretary Clinton took the MEK off the FTO list, the official view may have been that MEK actions in prior decades posed such a serious threat to US interests as to merit extraordinary caution before accepting the group's contention that it is non-violent today. Reporters and critics of the de-listing have highlighted notorious past terrorist events as key to understanding the MEK. To the historical dossier we now turn.

The April 1992 Worldwide 'Operation'.
The 2011 report says, *"In April 1992, the MEK conducted near-simultaneous attacks on Iranian embassies and consular missions in 13 countries, including against the Iranian mission to the United Nations in New York, demonstrating the group's ability to mount large-scale operations overseas."*

This episode, now more than 20 years past, has appeared in every version of *Country Reports* since 1993, with a mention of extensive property damage deleted after 1994. The specific reference to the attack on the Iranian mission in New York was, however, only added 19 years later in the 2010 report, issued under the stewardship of Counterterrorism Coordinator Daniel Benjamin. Mr. Benjamin touted this event in a press teleconference on July 6, 2012: *"The MEK is also one of the few foreign groups to attempt an attack on U.S. soil when, in 1992, it launched near-simultaneous attacks in 13 countries, including against the Iranian mission to the UN in New York."*[5] It was even mentioned in the State Department's September 28 de-listing announcement.

The public will be forgiven for envisioning a deadly conspiracy to cause mass casualties, in the mold of Al Qaeda, Baader-Meinhof, PFLP-GC and other violent extremist entities. The context of this event tells quite a different story.

On April 5, 1992, Iran violated the UN-mandated cease-fire from its 8-year war with Iraq, sending 13 F-4 fighter jets across the border, and bombed Camp Ashraf. Word of the bombing attack immediately spread to relatives and supporters worldwide, headlined with the news trumpeted by the regime's radio broadcast that day in Tehran (which turned out to be untrue) that MEK leader Massoud Rajavi had been killed. Diaspora MEK supporters converged on Iranian diplomatic missions in several countries and vented their rage, causing damage at a number of locations.

One of the Iranian jets, shot down in Iraq, was pictured the next day on page 1 of the *New York Times* (Figure 2). The caption reads in part, "Iranian jets bombed an Iranian rebel base in Iraq yesterday in the most serious attack by Iran since the 1988 cease-fire. ... In retaliation, opponents of Teheran invaded Iranian diplomatic missions in New York and elsewhere." CBC Radio of Canada, in a broadcast about the MEK on August 17, 2011, led with this statement: "On

Figure 2.
from *New York Times* front page, April 6, 1992.

April 5, 1992, a large group of Iranians attacked the Iranian Embassy in Ottawa. No one was seriously hurt, but the place was ransacked."[6]

The *Times* article said five men armed with knives "invaded" the Iranian mission to the UN, chained the doors detaining three "hostages" who were unharmed, "smashed furnishings and television and computer equipment and spray-painted anti-Government slogans on the walls ...." The story said one of the men, a resident of Queens, told the Associated Press by phone, "We are going to give ourselves up as soon as the press comes here. We have no weapons, believe me. I'm a man with a family."

No one involved in any of the attacks worldwide was charged with terrorism; none of the resulting court procedures anywhere alleged premeditation or centralized direction. The Canadian judge said that the protesters had reason to be angry.[7] What this incident showed was that MEK relatives and supporters around the world stayed in very close touch—presaging by 20 years the 'viral' communications phenomenon that has lately proven to be a potent engine for triggering public anger in many countries.

It certainly demonstrated that MEK supporters' hostility toward the rulers in Tehran could be provoked to the level of unruly, violent protest. That this incident continues to be held up twenty years later as a case of "*mount[ing] large-scale [terrorist] operations overseas*" suggests, at a minimum, that government analysis could profit from easier access to news media archives.

Notwithstanding the foregoing instances of mischaracterized events from recent years, most descriptions of the MEK look further back in history, to more serious alleged MEK acts of terrorism against the United States. Official US accounts of the three sets of 'historical crimes' are examined here:

Historical Crimes (I)—The Hostage Crisis. Perhaps no issue with Iran has shaped contemporary American attitudes more than the takeover of the American Embassy in Tehran on November 4, 1979 and the holding of 52 US hostages until the day of President Reagan's inauguration, January 20, 1981. From 1994 to 2005, the annual *Country Reports* said the MEK *"supported the takeover of the US Embassy in Tehran."* The 2006 report added the word *"violent"* to describe the Embassy takeover (one of 3 places *"violent"* was editorially inserted to augment existing descriptions of alleged activities in the 2005 and 2006 MEK reports). Finally, in the 2009 report, reference to the hostage crisis dropped out of the MEK dossier; government analysts apparently saw no MEK actions relating to the Embassy seizure that merited a mention 30 years after the fact. Yet, the very next year, in the 2010 report, the following lengthy passage appeared for the first time, repeated in the current (2011) edition: *"Though denied by the MEK, analysis based on eyewitness accounts and MEK documents demonstrates that MEK members participated in and supported the 1979 takeover of the US Embassy in Tehran and that the MEK later argued against the early release of the American hostages. The MEK also provided personnel to guard and defend the site of the U.S. Embassy in Tehran, following the takeover of the Embassy."*

This recent entry raises questions about whether the *Country Reports on Terrorism* is a straightforward factual resource or a more political document. According to the 2004 legal criteria for listing an entity as a FTO, a listed organization can demonstrate that the circumstances initially justifying its listing or re-listing have sufficiently changed that the FTO designation can be lifted after as little as two years; the Secretary of State is required by law not to let a designation exceed five years without reinvestigating the entity. What, then, is the significance of revisiting and embellishing the official view of MEK actions three decades after the fact? The further question arises whether fluctuating versions of history year-on-year reflect credible new information or have some other explanation.

Regardless of the State Department's evidence, there are certain historical truths about the MEK and the Embassy takeover of 1979 that will not be undermined by any particular piece of data. The Embassy seizure was instigated by a close-knit group of students from four universities looking to stage a three-day protest against American 'imperialist' influence over Iran. These devotees of Ayatollah Khomeini calling themselves "Muslim Students Following the Line of the Imam" coordinated their activities through Ayatollah Mohammed Mousavi Khoeiniha, who was their link to Khomeini. Once the students, exceeding their expectations, gained access to the entire Embassy compound including the shredded remnants of classified cables, and took the American diplomats hostage, the event became a global media sensation and the regime took full control. Three days became 444.

The Embassy crisis gave Khomeini and fellow hard-line clerics a windfall of popular support they used to consolidate power in Iran at the expense of the traditional organs of government under Prime Minister Mehdi Bazargan, a respected nationalist reformer, and other aspirants for a role in post-revolutionary Iran such as the MEK. Some MEK sympathizers were likely among the many thousands of Iranians who gathered outside the Embassy to revel in this spectacular act of defiance against the foreign superpower. Or perhaps eyewitness accounts from that episode referred to people from a different group bearing the Mujahedin label, such as the Mojahedin of Islamic Revolution *(Majehedin Enghelab Islami)* made up of Khomeini loyalists who went on to join the government or the Revolutionary Guards.

What is indisputable is that the political leverage the Embassy seizure handed to Khomeini directly undermined all of his political competitors including not just Prime Minister Bazargan and the 'civil' government but MEK leader Massoud Rajavi, who opposed replacing one dictatorship with another. In an October 20, 1984 interview with ABC News *Nightline*,

Rajavi denounced the action as a violation of diplomatic immunity. The same year, on the fifth anniversary of the Embassy takeover, Tehran Radio carried the speech of then-Chief Justice Ayatollah Abdul-Karim Mousavi Ardebili at the Embassy site, crediting the takeover with "the fall of the Provisional Government, the isolation of the liberals and the confusion of left-wing groups and the *Monafeqin* [MEK] ...." As the State Department notes, the MEK has always denied any role.

Massoumeh Ebtekar, at the time a 19-year-old student with good English skills who was part of the group that occupied the US Embassy and served as a spokesperson and translator for the hostage-holders, published a memoir 20 years later in Canada called *Takeover in Tehran—the Inside Story of the 1979 Embassy Capture*. She writes (p. 106), *"Many of our outside supporters may well have had friends in the [MEK], or even been sympathetic to them. Several [MEK] members had come over to the Muslim Students; when their leadership saw what had happened, they attempted to attach themselves to our movement. Back then, the dividing line had not yet been clearly drawn. It soon would be. Nonetheless, we had completely excluded the [MEK] and its members from participation in the Embassy occupation. Frustrated, they realized how much they could have benefited if only they could have become involved."*

Ms. Ebtekar—who later became a Vice President under President Mohammed Khatami—portrays the hostage-takers in a most favorable light, and her story is perhaps more useful as a window on their attitudes than as a factual reference.[8] Still, she describes (p. 174) Massoud Rajavi as a *"controversial figure who attempted to ingratiate himself with us .... [H]is followers phoned on his behalf asking for an appointment, which we immediately rejected. The Central Committee examined his request and voted unanimously to reject it. The decision was a blow to his campaign of self-promotion."* She also notes (p. 202) that when protection using armed patrols was deemed necessary, *"men from Sepah— Iran's newly-formed Revolutionary Guard corps—stood guard outside the walls."*

Professor Ervand Abrahamian of Baruch College, City University of New York, in his well-regarded 1989 scholarly history entitled *The Iranian Mojahedin*, cites (pp. 208–209) MEK publications at the time linking the hostage-takers to the mullahs' Islamic Republican Party and the *Pasdars* (Revolutionary Guards) and describing how the hard-line clerics had used the incident to "impose on the nation" their theocratic rule and "sweep aside" the civilian government.[9]

If observers today want to assign to the MEK a measure of enduring opprobrium for an alleged organized role in directing the 1979 Embassy takeover and perpetuating the hostage crisis, they must not only overcome evidence to the contrary, but offer a historically credible narrative. The recently-added US Government narrative does not meet this test. History clearly documents Massoud Rajavi's disadvantage from the radical clerics' power grab, and MEK members' longstanding regard for Prime Minister Bazargan, the liberal democratic nationalist who immediately resigned along with his cabinet in protest of the Embassy takeover.

Historical Crimes (II)—Bombings at American Sites in Iran. For the past three years, but not previously, the Department of State has included in its description of the MEK's alleged past activities a detailed paragraph covering events from 1972–1979 including setting off bombs at American official and corporate offices in Tehran. Setting off explosives is, by any definition, an extreme form of activism, but the way these incidents are now being portrayed and attributed by the US Government bears examination.

After the uprising of June 1963 when the Shah deployed military and police forces to attack, jail and silence political criticism, dissident political activity was forbidden and could be conducted only clandestinely as the repressive SAVAK intelligence service expanded its reach within the society. By the mid-1960s, two secret groups opposed to the government's repression and perceived subservience to Western powers—the *People's Mujahedin* (MEK) and the Marxist *Feda'iyan*—aspired to create in Iran the kind of 'post-colonial' liberation movement that had risen up against externally-supported elites in Algeria, Cuba and Vietnam among other developing countries at that time.

Professor Abrahamian, in his book, describes (p. 128) how the *Feda'iyan* gained wide notice by attacking a gendarmerie in February 1971, causing the MEK to accelerate its own timing for a spectacular act to embarrass the regime and puncture its aura of invincibility. With public events planned for August 1971 to commemorate 2,500 years of the monarchy, Abrahamian says the MEK *"decided to blow up the main electrical plant in Tehran and thus throw all the festivities into darkness."* However, in seeking a source for dynamite, the MEK used a contact who had turned informer. The attack was foiled.

Before the group could conduct any operations against the Shah's regime, over 100 MEK members were arrested, of whom 69 went on trial in early 1972. They included all eight original "Central Committee" members of the MEK including the three founders along with Massoud Rajavi, one of the youngest of the leaders, whose position stemmed from his strong intellect and writings influenced by an array of revolutionary and anti-colonial political thinkers. All of these MEK leaders but Rajavi were executed. The latter's sentence was commuted to life imprisonment after his older brother in Geneva arranged for prominent foreign personages, including François Mitterrand and Jean Paul Sartre, to ask that he be spared.

Only at this trial did the existence of the MEK as an organization, and its name, become known to the authorities; it had been kept secret for six years. The MEK's activity from its inception had focused on publishing and disseminating political and sociological critiques of Iran under the Shah, and its program of resistance. At their trials, condemned MEK leaders addressed the military tribunal, criticizing the regime's repressive rule and its dependence on US support as they faced death with defiance and equanimity.

Some of these speeches were smuggled out of prison and externally circulated. Among Iranian student populations in America as well as inside Iran, the *'Mujahedin'* (the full name translated means 'The People's Crusaders') gained a measure of prestige for risking and losing their lives while standing up to the Shah's repression. The MEK's stance had many sympathizers among the clerics as well (although Khomeini withheld his support).

Surviving MEK members sought to regroup and carry on the 'struggle.' But who were they? As much of the MEK leadership had been killed, or imprisoned like Massoud Rajavi, other members of the group staged operations against the regime and threatened further activities in an effort to compel the release of their jailed comrades. These operations by the remaining MEK probably included some attacks directed against US sites in Iran highlighted in the three most recent editions of the *Country Reports*.

What the reports do not mention about these attacks 40 years ago is that, as Abrahamian writes (p. 140), *"Throughout these years, the Mojahedin tended to set off their bombs late at night and after telephone warnings in order to limit civilian casualties. ... None of these incidents were considered worth mentioning by the US press."* Nor was the MEK the only entity to which these actions could be attributed: the *Feda'iyan*, Abrahamian says, was also staging bombing attacks in protest against the US. He adds (p. 143), *"To counter their 'propaganda by deed,' the [Shah's] regime waged its own propaganda campaign against both the Mojahedin and the Feda'iyan. ... The regime claimed that the shoot-outs and bombings caused heavy casualties among bystanders and innocent civilians, especially women and children .... It obtained 'public confessions' from 'repentant guerrillas' accusing their former colleagues of a host of crimes ...."*

The reality would seem to be that the MEK in the early 1970s was among dissident groups that set off explosives at sites in Iran associated with the Shah's security institutions and the United States in order to tarnish the image of stability promoted by the Iranian government with the public, foreign governments and multinational corporations. The gravity of these actions—which, to be clear, were illegal, dangerous and anti-American— was nevertheless inflated by the Shah's regime at the time. Still unexplained is why these incidents assumed new prominence in the US Government's MEK terrorism dossier so many years later.

Historical Crimes (III)—The Killing of Americans in Iran in the 1970s. The most damning allegation of all against the MEK, repeated in the de-listing announcement, in every edition of the *Country Reports* through the years, and in virtually every press article and commentary on the MEK, is that the assassinations of six American officials and contractors in Iran in the 1970s were the work of *"the MEK."*

The problem with this statement is that it is not the whole truth, as a result of which the allegation is levied against individuals and groups of people who are not responsible for these grave offenses against the United States. The killings were in some sense the work of "MEK" members. But applied to members, supporters and sympathizers of today's MEK—indeed, of the MEK since the early 1970s—this allegation is unsupportable, one could even say false.

As will be seen, 'pinning' the murders on the current MEK that revived in 1978–79 under Massoud Rajavi's leadership is a bit like holding Palestinian Authority officials and supporters responsible for past killings by early members of Hamas because both entities emerged from the Palestinian resistance to Israel's occupation. The killings of Americans in Iran in the early-to-mid 1970s were the work not of people now associated with the MEK, but rather their rivals among dissident elements opposing the Shah.

Start with an egregious error in the Department of State's *Country Reports*, repeated in the 2009, 2010 and 2011 editions. Of the period after Khomeini took power in 1979, it says: *"[T]he MEK's ideology ... was at odds with the post-revolutionary government, and its original leadership was soon executed by the Khomeini regime."* That the US Government has, for three years at least, been operating under the belief that the MEK's "original leadership" was alive throughout the 1970s, and put to death by Khomeini's regime after the 1979 revolution rather than by the Shah's regime in early 1972, is more than a typo or minor slip. It is a fundamental factual blunder.

By the time the killing of Americans in Iran began in 1973—indeed, more than a year before—many members of the original MEK including all of the founding MEK leadership had been executed or killed by the Shah's security forces, and Massoud Rajavi was in prison where he would remain until January 1979.

Remarkably, the State Department also exhibits confusion about numbers even when referring to the murders of US citizens. While Ambassador Benjamin, until December 2012 the Department of State's Counterterrorism Coordinator, in public remarks cited seven as the number of Americans assassinated in Iran during the 1970s, the most recent four iterations of the *Country Reports on Terrorism* list only six. The 2008, 2009, 2010 and 2011 reports count only two American employees of Rockwell International as having been killed in 1976, even though press reports at the time and a 1994 State Department report (see below) said there had been three. These recent versions of the *Country Reports* feature a new allegation that, *"In 1979, the group claimed responsibility for the murder of an American Texaco executive,"* a statement the MEK says is untrue.

The identities of the assassins of American military advisors and contractors in Tehran are known. The *Washington Post* story on May 11, 1976 reported (p. A9) that in January of that year, *"nine terrorists convicted of murdering the three American colonels … were executed by firing squad. The leader of the group, Vahid Afrakhteh, told a Westerner allowed to see him shortly before his execution that …. he personally killed Col. Lewis Hawkins in Tehran in 1973 and led the cell that gunned down Col. Paul Shaffer and Lt. Col. Jack Turner after stopping their … car in 1975."* A UPI story dated November 16, 1976, carried the following day in the *Post*, reported that the Tehran police had shot and killed Bahram Aram, *"the man who masterminded the August slayings"* of three Americans working for Rockwell International.

Despite the availability of this information, a 1994 Department of State report on the MEK prepared for Congress erred in purporting to name MEK perpetrators of three of the six killings of Americans that took place from 1973–76. (However, this report did correctly name the six assassinated Americans including three, not two, Rockwell International employees; no mention was made of the 1979 murder of a Texaco executive.) It incorrectly stated that MEK member Reza Reza'i had been arrested and executed for the 1973 murder of Lt. Colonel Lewis L. Hawkins. In fact, Reza'i had been arrested in 1971 with other leading MEK members, and escaped from prison; government security forces killed him in 1973 in a standoff in Tehran. This same report names "Rahman Vahid Afrakhteh" as the killer of the other two US military officers, incorrectly conflating the names of two brothers, Rahman and Vahid Afrakhteh.

Even though the murderers of the Americans were known to US security agencies dating back to the mid-1970s, when the Western press reported that nine members of the breakaway Marxist faction had been caught and executed after having confessed to the killings, the 2006 *Country Reports,* issued in April 2007, made a curious assertion not included before or since: *"Despite U.S. efforts, MEK members have never been brought to justice for the group's role in these illegal acts."* A report by a former political prisoner circulated on Iranian web sites claims that one member of Vahid Afrakhteh's team that conducted the assassinations of three Americans survived and took up residence in Europe. However, the author has found no indication in the public literature that US authorities ever pursued such an individual for acts of terrorism against the US.

The real assassins of Americans in Iran, including Vahid Afrakhteh and Bahram Aram, were part of a faction that emerged from the remnants of the MEK following the execution and imprisonment of many leading MEK members in 1972, and ultimately split away entirely (and violently) in 1975. This group adopted a more secular, extremist and doctrinaire leftist identity; they were not committed to Islam as a defining interest. Known initially as the Mujahedin M.L. (for "Marxist-Leninist") and later as the "Iranian People's Strugglers for the Working Class (Peykar)," the group had ties to George Habash and the PFLP as well as secessionists in Oman and possibly the Cuban government.

The MEK split, which originated in 1972 and became widely apparent by 1975, was real. Iran's leading center of technical education, originally known as Arya Mehr Industrial University, was renamed Sharif University following the 1979 revolution to honor Majid Sharif-Vaqefi, by 1975 a leader of the surviving MEK. He had defended the Islamic identity of the group against the challenge by hard-line secular leftists.

On May 7, 1975, Sharif-Vaqefi was killed in an operation planned by the leaders of the Marxist splinter group, including both Vahid Afrahkteh and Bahram Aram as well as Taghi Shahram. Another Muslim MEK leader of the day, Mohammed Yaqini, was also killed by this breakaway group. A third, Morteza Samadiyeh Labbaf, was shot and wounded by this breakaway faction; apprehended by the Shah's SAVAK security service,

> a.k.a. MKO;
> Mujahedin-e Khalq;
> Muslim Iranian Students' Society;
> National Council of Resistance;
> National Council of Resistance (NCR);
> Organization of the People's Holy Warriors of Iran;
> The National Liberation Army of Iran (NLA);
> The People's Mujahedin Organization of Iran (PMOI);
> National Council of Resistance of Iran (NCRI);
> Sazeman-e Mujahedin-e Khalq-e Iran
>
> **Description**
> The MEK advocates the violent overthrow of the Iranian regime. The MEK philosophy mixes Marxism, feminism, nationalism, and Islam. The group emerged as one of several political movements seeking to unseat the Shah in 1960s. After Khomeini's regime arrested most of the MEK leadership a few years after the Islamic Revolution, m members fled to Europe. Saddam Hussein invited the group to Iraq in the late 1980s, where it reformed as a paramilitary organization and conducted several cross-border forays into Iran. A Marxist element of the MEK murdered several of the Shah's U.S. security advisers prior to the Islamic Revolution, and the group helped gua U.S. Embassy after Islamic students seized it in 1979. Since then, the MEK has conducted terrorist attacks aga the interests of the clerical regime in Iran and abroad.

Figure 3.
Country Reports on Terrorism 2005, from Department of State website.

Labbaf was tortured before being executed by a firing squad.

In prison, Massoud Rajavi, after learning of these events, wrote a book during the latter half of the 1970s critical of these "pseudo-leftist opportunists," their "ideologically transformed organization," and their military operations that had killed US citizens in their bid to "challenge" and outmaneuver the "genuine" (meaning Muslim) MEK.

In 2005, the Department of State correctly attributed the murders of Americans in Iran to this breakaway secular group; the *Country Reports* for that year, issued on April 28, 2006, said, "*A Marxist element of the MEK murdered several of the Shah's U.S. security advisers prior to the Islamic Revolution ...*" (Figure 3) This more precise historical attribution, fully cleared by US agencies for inclusion in the 2005 *Country Reports*, was excised from subsequent editions, without explanation.

In addressing this, the most enduring and prejudicial of all the allegations against the MEK, the official narrative obscures the most important truth: Massoud Rajavi, and the revived MEK under his leadership from the late 1970s onward, had no involvement in the killings of Americans in Iran. Those acts were the work of rivals who broke away from the MEK, most if not all of whom were either apprehended and executed after confessing to the murders, or killed in clashes with government security forces. The possibility that any person affiliated with today's MEK was connected to the assassinations of Americans in Iran during the 1970s is all but nonexistent.

A footnote is in order regarding the frequent use of "Marxist" to describe the MEK's beliefs; the 2011 *Country Reports* used the term three times–"*Marxist-Islamic*", "*Marxists*" and "*Marxism.*" While the political writings by founding MEK members drew on Marx's sociological critique of class inequality, they flatly rejected Marx's political ideology. Members of the extremist element that broke away from the MEK in the early-to-mid 1970s were, by contrast, self-proclaimed Marxists.

As one academic who has studied MEK ideology (but is no MEK supporter), Syracuse University Professor Mehrzad Boroujerdi, has written, Massoud Rajavi and the MEK *"hoped to challenge the vigorous presence of Marxism within Iranian intellectual circles. The group remained skeptical of Marxism's postulates and rejected ... historical materialism"* while maintaining their religious beliefs.[10] Abrahamian writes (p. 2), *"The [MEK] has in fact never once used the terms socialist, communist, Marxist or eshteraki [Communist] to describe itself."* Nor has the MEK ever had an office in a Communist country.

However, both the Shah's and the clerics' regimes saw advantage in attaching a Marxist label to the MEK. Abrahamian again (p. 101): *"As [Massoud] Rajavi admitted years later, the organization avoided the socialist label because such a term conjured up in the public mind images of atheism, materialism, and Westernism. For exactly the same reasons, the [Shah's] regime was eager to pin on the [MEK] the label of Islamic-Marxists and Marxist-Muslims."* Rajavi told *Time* magazine in September 1981, *"[F]or dictators like Khomeini, 'Marxist Islamic' is a very profitable phrase to use against any opposition. If Jesus Christ and Muhammad were alive and protesting against Khomeini, he would call them Marxists, too."*[11]

1980 — The Lost Year

Reviewing these and other discrepancies between official accounts and historical reality, it is hard not to wonder how differently the MEK and its history might be perceived today in Washington had US diplomats not been held captive from November 1979 to January 1981 (Figure 4). Not only were America's premier linguists and experts on Iranian affairs prevented from witnessing and reporting on the many ways that Ayatollah Khomeini, his agents and loyalists sidelined Prime Minister Bazargan and then President Bani-Sadr while

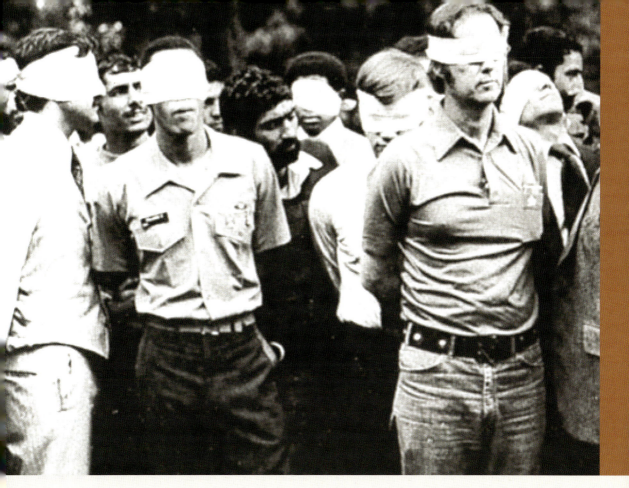

Figure 4.
US hostages in Iran, 1979, © Bettmann/Corbis

suppressing Massoud Rajavi's campaign and those of other political factions for long-denied popular sovereignty; but America's attention was one hundred percent glued to the fate of the hostages—understandably so—and not at all attuned to political jostling for power inside Iran following the Shah's demise.

This gap in America's collective historical memory is fateful. What happened during this time defined the fundamentalist Islamic regime's claim to power and planted the seeds of its vulnerability. The end of the monarchy precipitated an intense competition across the political spectrum for public support, answered by obstruction, escalating threats and violence from the clerics. The elevated expectations of many Iranians for a modern democracy after the 1979 revolution were denied as Khomeini supplanted the Shah's harsh security state with new organs reimposing firm control under the banner of higher religious authority. In reaction to the mullahs' aggressive actions, a second 'revolution' was materializing throughout the country by the spring of 1981, and might well have upended Khomeini's consolidation of power had he and his circle not massively deployed their new instruments of repression to stop it at all costs.

Possibly no misrepresentation in the entire official history of the MEK's activities stands out more than this passage in the current (2011) *Country Reports:* "*In 1981, MEK leadership attempted to overthrow the newly installed Islamic regime; Iranian security forces subsequently initiated a crackdown on the group. The MEK instigated a bombing campaign … which killed some 70 high-ranking Iranian officials …. These attacks resulted in an expanded Iranian government crackdown that forced MEK leaders to flee to France.*" This narrative, standing the truth on its head, creates a clear sequence placing the moral onus for having resorted first to violent measures on the MEK and Massoud Rajavi, while labeling his political campaign as an attempted "overthrow." The longer-term implication is clear: whatever grief may have befallen MEK members and sympathizers from 1981 onward was their own fault; the group provoked the clerics, who were justified in responding with tough measures.

The State Department has not always interpreted 1980-81 this way; in fact, the words quoted above first appeared only five years earlier, in the 2006 *Country Reports*, issued in April 2007—an edition containing several questionable new passages on the MEK examined in this study. The versions issued during the previous dozen years dating to 1993, had merely said this: "*In the 1980s, the MEK's leaders were forced by Iranian security forces to flee to France.*" The rewriting of history about a pivotal episode 26 years after the fact would be appropriate were it done in the interest of greater accuracy and based on improved historical data. As will be seen below, that rationale is absent in this case.

To grasp the impact of the 'lost year' of political reporting, it is worth considering some of the developments that went overlooked in Washington as US officials dealt first with the controversial issue of admitting the exiled Shah to the US for cancer treatment and then the Embassy hostage crisis in which the hostage-holders demanded that the US return the Shah to face justice in Iran. Massoud Rajavi, released from jail in January 1979, traveled to Qom in September to meet with Ayatollah Khomeini, whose executive, legislative and judicial authority relative to the civilian government had not yet been defined. A long-time MEK member who accompanied Rajavi to that meeting described it to the author.

He said that three years earlier, a memo Massoud Rajavi had written in prison to other MEK members warning that "reactionary mullahs" posed the biggest threat to the revolution, had reached Khomeini. Nevertheless, Khomeini had welcomed Rajavi and said "You have done a lot; but as you know the main issue between us is Islam. We must do whatever we can to ensure Islam reigns supreme in Iran." Khomeini asked Rajavi to collaborate against leftists, minorities and Kurdish separatists whom he collectively termed 'counter-revolutionaries.' He asked that Rajavi accept the terms of the Iranian Revolution, reflected in the constitutional referendum to be held in early December 1979.

Rajavi's response was that "We are Muslims; but the first message of Islam is 'freedom.'" Khomeini's smile, said this witness, turned cold and he looked down angrily, avoiding further eye contact with his visitors. Rajavi continued that the people expected leaders to adhere to the slogans of the revolution, but Khomeini only said goodbye. The word 'freedom' had ended the discussion.

From early 1979 through June 1981, Rajavi and the MEK engaged in open political activity while avoiding confrontation with the clerics. For their part, the 'shadow government' institutions forming around Khomeini, including street gangs *(Hezbollahis)* made up of Khomeini loyalists, sought to blunt their campaign with threats, harassment of political rallies, and destructive attacks on MEK offices and printing presses around the country.

Rajavi campaigned for President saying he would improve on Khomeini's constitution which was based on *Velayat-e faqih* (guardianship of the Islamic jurist) and amounted to dictatorship. Writing in 1981, George W. Ball, who had been Under Secretary of State and then US Ambassador to the UN under Presidents Kennedy and Johnson, commented that the MEK's *"intention is to replace the current backward Islamic regime with a modernized Shiite Islam drawing its egalitarian principles from Koranic sources rather than Marx."*[12]

Khomeini banned Rajavi and other MEK candidates for office on the basis of their refusal to support his new constitution. *Le Monde*'s correspondent wrote on March 29, 1980 that Rajavi would have received *"several million votes"* including support from *"religious and ethnic minorities… a good part of the female vote… and the young"* had his candidacy not been disallowed. Abolhasan Bani-Sadr became Iran's first elected President in February 1980.

Rajavi ran for Parliament, receiving about 500,000 votes, as did Maryam Azodanlu (later Maryam Rajavi) who received about 250,000 votes. Other MEK candidates polled strongly, but all were disqualified by the clerics from taking office. At some point in early 1980, Khomeini issued a hand-written judicial order to execute MEK members and

Figure 5. ▶
Demonstration by estimated 500,000 MEK supporters in Tehran, June 20, 1981.
Courtesy MEK

supporters.[13] Regime forces ransacked every office printing or distributing the MEK journal *Mojahed*, which was driven into hiding by late 1980 to keep publishing. Public rhetoric between the MEK and the mullahs became more confrontational. Attacks by *Hezbollahis* injured and killed many MEK supporters.

In July of 1980, the regime foiled an extensive plot by military and former security service officers operating from several bases in Iran to overthrow the clerics and stave off their budding dictatorship. Known as the 'Nojeh coup,' this episode reflected the depth of popular concern about Iran's post-Revolution direction under Ayatollah Khomeini. While the military had pursued the route of *coup d'état*, the MEK continued its political activities, appealing for public support.

As major Western newspapers reported from Tehran, Rajavi drew crowds in the tens of thousands to his speeches despite escalating threats, injuries and arrests. A protest rally on April 27, 1981, grew to over 150,000 according to Abrahamian (pp. 216–7). The regime banned all future MEK demonstrations. The MEK wrote an open letter to President Bani-Sadr asking the government to protect the citizens' "right to demonstrate peacefully." As Abrahamian put it, "Clearly, the regime was losing control on the streets." (Contrast that to the 2006 *Country Reports* with its newly-inserted language, which said, *"Following [the MEK's] participation in the 1979 Islamic Revolution, the group rapidly fell out of favor with the Iranian people."*)

June 20, 1981 would be the pivotal date of this entire period. On June 19, says Abrahamian (p. 218), Rajavi and President Bani-Sadr together had "called upon the whole nation to take over the streets the next day to express their opposition to the [regime] 'monopolists' who they claimed had carried out a secret *coup d'etat*." An outpouring of people materialized the next day in cities across the country—half a million in the streets of Tehran alone (Figure 5).

The Mujahedin-e Khalq (MEK)

Faced with the prospect of being swept aside by a second revolution not unlike the one he had ridden to prominence two years earlier as the Shah's rule collapsed, Khomeini moved to impeach Bani-Sadr the next day. His regime arrested and executed several close allies of both Rajavi and Bani-Sadr, forcing the two men into hiding, and launched what Abrahamian calls (p. 219) "a reign of terror unprecedented in modern Iranian history."

The question of who provoked whom—whose actions were the more legitimate—in this struggle for Iran's future is neither muddled nor complicated. The clerics, faced with increasingly successful political competition, resorted to escalating force to secure their monopoly of power. The granting to himself of divine powers by Khomeini, imposed through new religious courts and militias, was challenged by the nationwide political campaigns of his opponents, supporters of the traditional institutions of government, who were attacked and either killed or arrested, or driven into hiding. Abrahamian says (p. 213) that by the time of the June 20, 1981 rally, i.e., before the MEK went underground and turned to violent tactics, regime attacks had already killed 71 MEK members and supporters—as many as had died in the prior seven years of resistance to the Shah's regime.

The State Department version of history, at least as portrayed since 2007, entirely skips over Khomeini's year-long descent to bloody dictatorship. The MEK and a handful of other organized political groups are held responsible for the resort to force, when the very opposite was the case. They are labeled as the extremists and aggressors because they turned to clandestine armed resistance after June 20, 1981, never mind that hundreds among them were daily being rounded up into prison and shot in the streets. Rajavi along with Bani-Sadr—the elected President of the country, it bears reminding—went into hiding together, with the latter under MEK protection. Both escaped probable death when they were smuggled onto a plane and flown to Paris by an Iranian Air Force Colonel on July 28, 1981.

With MEK members and sympathizers, and other political challengers to Khomeini, being hunted and summarily executed by the clerics' enforcers, on June 28, 1981 a bomb killed and wounded a number of senior regime clerics, among them Chief Justice Ayatollah Mohammad Hossein Beheshti, gathered at their party conference in Tehran. The Department of State's account of this bombing cites "some 70" regime officials as having been killed. This US estimate is almost surely wrong. Some unofficial accounts put the correct number of those killed closer to 120; the regime's figure of 73—Beheshti "plus 72"—was, by these accounts, a public relations creation intended to conjure popular association with the epic battle of Karbala in 680 A.D. when the Third Imam of Shi'ism, Imam Hussein, is said to have perished heroically along with 72 others fighting a much larger force.

This detail of the casualty count is noted to illustrate the regime's capacity to confect facts to suit its political agenda. According to the Reuters dispatch in the *New York Times* on June 30, 1981, the authorities initially blamed the "Great Satan" (the US); Abrahamian (p. 220) noted that the regime also suspected "SAVAK survivors and the Iraqi regime." The Nationalist Equality Party, an Iranian resistance group in Turkey, claimed credit for the attack, according to the *Times* story. The pro-Soviet Tudeh party was also suspected. The newspaper further noted that the evening before, on June 27, a bomb had exploded inside a tape recorder, permanently injuring the right arm of Ali Khamenei, now Iran's Supreme Leader; according to the *Times* account, "a note had been found saying the *Forghan* group, which opposes the involvement of clergy in politics, had staged the attack …."

Within days, the regime shifted its story and blamed the MEK. Throughout its 30 years of underground armed resistance the MEK habitually issued communiqués taking credit for its actions against the regime, yet it never claimed responsibility for the June 28, 1981 bombing. The Tudeh party, the Turkey-based Nationalist Equality Party and *Forghan* were all opposition groups repressed by the clerical regime who were capable of such an action. Another was the Iranian military, blamed for this attack by ex-President Bani-Sadr years later in exile. Still, the State Department has, since 2002, listed this bombing in the MEK dossier.

The difference between the documented history of this seminal period in Iran's political development and the narrative one finds today in Washington is substantial and important. The MEK was in 1980–81 a thriving nationalist movement that, having paid dearly in the Shah's jails for its beliefs, was unwilling to put aside its central objective of achieving popular sovereignty in deference to Khomeini's totalitarian project. As Professor Abrahamian puts it (p. 209), "*In criticizing the regime's political record, the Mojahedin moved the issue of democracy to centre stage. They argued that … the issue of democracy was of 'fundamental importance' ….*" Yet this reality is lost in the official portrayal of the MEK as a secretive and congenitally violent group with obscure beliefs and social values alien to civilized norms.

We are asked to accept that the MEK sealed its own unhappy fate by violently disrupting the post-revolutionary order in 1981, provoking the forceful security measures that drove its surviving members underground or out of Iran altogether. We are not invited to ponder the merits or tactics of the mullahs' path to absolute control in Iran, as Americans are wont to do with political developments in virtually every country. If, as Abraham Lincoln said, "History is not history unless it is the truth," there is much room for correction of the existing official account, and Americans can hope for an improved understanding of these protagonists, their goals and their actions, the better to render informed judgments.

The Correct Analytical Lens: Conflict, Not Terrorism

What remains when one clears away the false, mischaracterized and unsupported pieces of the MEK terrorism dossier? The Department of State's report will still contain periods of violent MEK activity, much of it openly claimed by the organization at the time. The most active periods were the early 1970s as noted above, the few years after June 1981, the latter part of the 1980s, and the latter part of the 1990s until about 2001. These activities reflect two characteristics that do not fit the mold of counterterrorism analysis: first, the violence was targeted almost without exception against the state, meaning Iranian regime officials, security forces, buildings, etc.; and second, all of these actions occurred in the context of ongoing two-way conflict between the MEK and the regime enforcers of the Shah and later the ruling mullahs.

Both features of this 'corrected' dossier—the focus on Iranian regime targets, and the context of a two-way conflict between the MEK and the regime's agents—are obscured when one views MEK activity solely through the specialized prism of "terrorism." A terrorist group is by nature prone to gratuitous, indiscriminate violence, and is content—even eager—to harm innocents. Such actions are unjustifiable by any recognized standard no matter what their perpetrators' beliefs or grievances may be. When a group is waging unprovoked attacks on innocent people, the public is not obliged to consider the root causes of its disaffection.

The MEK's record, however, suggests a different ethical calculus, even though it employed violent means in opposition to Iran's rulers for much of the time between 1971 and 2001. As recorded in the *Daily Hansard* proceedings of the British House of Lords on March 27, 2001, MEK leader Massoud Rajavi had said in 2000, *"I pledge on behalf of the Iranian resistance that if anyone from our side oversteps the red line concerning absolute prohibition of attacks on civilians and innocent individuals, either deliberately or unintentionally, he or she would be ready to stand trial in any international court and accept any ruling by the court, including the payment of compensation."*[14]

The resort to armed resistance by the MEK may be criticized in hindsight, but it happened for a reason. One need not share the group's identification with the century-old nationalist movement or the mid-century liberation movement to acknowledge that power and privilege have long been highly concentrated in Iran, and that popular aspirations for reform—emanating from many points on the political spectrum—have repeatedly been met by force.

The security forces of the Shah and the clerics, respectively, pursued their political critics with extreme brutality, successfully intimidating and silencing most opposition. The MEK has always consisted of educated Iranians who stood by their commitment, inspired by decades of unrealized nationalist hopes, to rid the country of corrupt and dictatorial government. The group's record of anti-regime activity has not only been embellished with false and distorted information, but also judged in isolation, devoid of context. There are two sides to this conflict.

If the MEK's role in this conflict—its members' refusal to accept the legitimacy of the clerics' claim to power after 1979—is troubling to some Americans, they might reflect on the fact that the US Government has also withheld formal recognition and acceptance of the Iranian revolution over the same period.

The original MEK was a discussion group secretly formed in 1965 by three Tehran University graduates, Mohammed Hanifnejad, Saeed Mohsen and Ali Ashgar Badizadegan, who were active in (later Prime Minister) Bazargan's Freedom Movement. Hanifnejad and

Mohsen had been jailed in 1963 because of campus protests calling for social justice. For six years they studied ways to apply other developing country experiences that they believed would mobilize popular support to unseat an illegitimate ruling class in Iran.

Later, the revived MEK led from 1979 on by Massoud Rajavi campaigned openly and peacefully, as noted, in opposition to Ayatollah Khomeini's bid for fundamentalist dictatorship. Driven into exile, Rajavi told the French weekly *L'Humanité* on January 2, 1984, *"If Khomeini is prepared to hold truly free elections, I will return to my homeland immediately. The [MEK] will lay down their arms to participate in such elections."*

However, as with the Shah, Ayatollah Khomeini's only response to the MEK's political challenge was overwhelming force, and the two camps clashed for the next 20 years. In 2001 the MEK unilaterally embarked on a purely political track, disarming completely two years later, but it remained dedicated to the same beliefs and political goals, all the more so in recognition of how many among them had lost their lives for those beliefs.

The dearth of analytical focus on the Iranian state's activities against the MEK leaves out another crucial aspect of the story: the extent of, and reason for, the clerical regime's fear of this opposition group, arguably above all others. The regime's obsession with the MEK is about neither terrorism nor ideology, but religious legitimacy. Unlike the *Feda'iyan*, Tudeh party, Peykar and other organized opposition groups, MEK members are Muslims, and the group has always stood for the proposition that Islam embodies individual rights for men and women alike, respects other faiths, and is fully compatible with modern living and higher education.

Professor Shaul Bakhash has written that after the 1979 revolution Khomeini was *"suspicious of the Mojahedin's growing strength and disapproved of their attempts, as laymen, to appropriate to themselves the authority to interpret Islamic doctrine."*[15] In exile during the 1980s the MEK instituted gender equality, a concept unheard of even today in Muslim societies, as a rebuke to the clerics' repression of women. Today hundreds of MEK women are empowered and coequal to men in the organization. Such a modern view of Islam directly challenges the *Velayat-e Faqih* doctrine investing the Supreme Leader with divine authority that the mullahs, since the revolution, have parlayed into religious, social and political dominion over the population.

The MEK's story, in sum, is a case study of political conflict, not terrorism. It is at its core a contest with the ruling powers in Iran over political rights, legitimacy and power. Had peaceful political dissent been permitted by the Shah in the early 1960s and the mullahs after 1979, there is no reason to believe the MEK would ever have gone underground or embraced the path of armed resistance. Its vision of social and political evolution in Iran, expressed in speeches and writings, was always the MEK's *raison d'être* and source of appeal. As will be seen, US Government experts a generation ago grasped these central truths about the MEK.

The fact that Iran's rulers have for so long denied the population any political 'space' for dissent or democratic participation, and have answered their critics with imprisonment and death, accounts for Iran's tragic descent into violence over the past half century. Observers can judge the relative guilt or innocence, right or wrong of the protagonists in this grim conflict. No party, including the MEK, is above criticism. But in Washington, the beginning of wisdom will be to recognize that the MEK's activities over time, and the actions of those in power in Tehran, were always intimately connected, and are best understood when viewed side by side.

Trade Bait: 25 Years as a Diplomatic Commodity

One recurring connection between the MEK and the Iranian government is found in the long history of diplomatic 'horse-trading' between Tehran and Western capitals, where Iran's willingness to cooperate on critical security issues was made contingent on other governments' readiness to take enforcement actions to restrict the MEK. The charge has often been made in Washington by the MEK's advocates that its original designation as a FTO in 1997 by Secretary of State Madeleine Albright was intended as a goodwill gesture to the newly-elected government of Mohammed Khatami, with the hope of encouraging moderation by Iran.[16] Critics labeled this action "appeasement of the mullahs" that failed to deliver the hoped-for result; and indeed, before leaving office, Khatami presided over the development of Iran's then-secret nuclear program.

1985-86: US-Iran	Tower Commission Report on Iran-Contra affair includes 5-page letter to a regime contact from Manucher Ghorbanifar citing the *"[Issuance] of an official announcement terming the [MEK] terrorist and Marxist"* as one of several US steps taken *"as a sign of goodwill"*; the Assistant Secretary of State for Near Eastern Affairs had volunteered such a statement at a 1985 congressional hearing. The apparent purpose was to win the release of American hostages held in Lebanon.
1986: France-Iran	Massoud Rajavi and many exiled followers in Paris were expelled by France's government led by Prime Minister Jacques Chirac, in exchange for Iran's arranging the release of French hostages held in Lebanon. Although Chirac had hoped for the return of six hostages, only two were released. It was this French-Iranian understanding that led to the MEK seeking refuge in Iraq, where it remains over a quarter-century later.
1987: France-Iran	The Chirac government made a second attempt to gain the release of French hostages in Iran when it agreed to deport the remaining MEK from France to Gabon. MEK members fearing that they would be returned to Iran against their will, staged a 40-day hunger strike, creating such controversy that Chirac had to ask Saddam Hussein to request Massoud Rajavi's assistance in negotiating with the exiles; they were allowed to remain in France.
1997: US-Iran	A top policy aide to Secretary of State Albright confirmed that the US listing of the MEK as a terrorist group had been done as a gesture of goodwill to newly-elected President Mohammed Khatami of Iran, in the hopes of improved relations.
1999: US-Iran	US officials confirmed that the addition of MEK aliases and the NCRI (the MEK's political umbrella) to its FTO designation had been at Iran's request.
2000: UK-Iran	UK Foreign Minister Robin Cook reached agreement with his Iranian counterpart : he characterized MEK as a terrorist group in a joint press conference; in return Iran agreed not to enforce its *fatwa* against Salman Rushdie, then living in UK
2003: France-Iran	French law enforcement authorities arrested MEK political leadership and staff in Paris as a "deliverable" in an arrangement involving award by Iran of an oil contract to *Total* arranged between the two countries' Foreign Ministers.
2003: US/UK- Iran	US officials meeting with Iranian officials in Geneva explicitly agreed that MEK sites would be targeted by US forces in Operation Iraqi Freedom, in return for which Iran would not interfere with OIF; UK Foreign Secretary Jack Straw confirmed the arrangement with Iranian Foreign Minister Kharrazi. Even though the MEK in Iraq had declared it was neutral and would play no role, and had supplied coordinates for its locations to the UN and Coalition forces, US forces bombed Camp Ashraf.
2003: US-Iran	Top officials contemplated a 'swap' under which the US would offer to turn over the more than 3,000 MEK exiles in Iraq to the custody of Iran, in return for which Iran would hand over to the US the relatives of Osama bin Laden believed to be resident inside Iran under the regime's protection. The deal was not pursued with Iran reportedly because some in the Bush Administration were opposed to any positive cooperation with Tehran.
2004: EU-Iran	EU-3 (French, German and British) diplomats negotiating with Iran on the nuclear issue agreed to include in a joint communique a shared commitment between the EU and Iran to *"combat … the activities of … terrorist groups such as the MEK"* and to do so *"irrespective of progress on the nuclear issue …."*
2006: UK-Iran	UK Foreign Minister Jack Straw told BBC Radio that he had agreed to a request from Iran's Foreign Minister to put the MEK on the UK's terrorism list.

Figure 6.
US and European diplomacy with Tehran with 'deliverables' involving the MEK.

As distasteful as it may be for diplomats to hear themselves labeled cynical and perhaps naïve in trading on the welfare of these dissident exiles in hopes of receiving various *quids pro quo* from the most prolific state supporter of terrorism, a review of the past quarter-century should give some comfort to Secretary Albright, for she is in very good company. Not only American but French, British and German governments negotiated with Tehran at the MEK's expense, to say nothing of Iraq, which since 2008 has made no effort to conceal its collusion with Tehran against the MEK. The 2003 vignette described above involving French Foreign Minister Villepin was but one of many instances where US or European 'counterterrorism' measures against the MEK were a form of compensation to Iran linked to other equities.

This is not a matter of one or two isolated instances. Diplomatic transactions with Tehran affecting the MEK spanning more than two decades are summarized in Figure 6.

With the Department of State's September 2012 confirmation that the MEK committed no terrorism during the past decade, it is fair to wonder whether at any time—beginning with its initial listing in 1997, or thereafter—the MEK was objectively assessed to be a terrorist group posing a threat to US interests, like other listed terrorist groups. So persistent have been Tehran's private demands for other governments to take action against the group that the burden of proof surely rests with those governments to dispel the impression that all such designations of the MEK by the US, Europe, Iraq and even Canada and Australia were traceable to diplomatic leverage exerted by the Iranian government.

Terrorists or Not, Bizarre and Cruel People: The RAND and Human Rights Watch Reports

If, as the State Department says,[17] FTO designations are a *"means of … pressuring groups to get out of the terrorism business,"* the MEK's de-listing should be regarded as a US policy achievement. Yet no sense of accomplishment marked the US Government's pronouncements regarding the MEK's official exit from "the terrorism business." Why not?

Some entities are listed as FTOs on the basis of recent terror activity; some have a long history of terrorist actions. The MEK has for the past 15 years faced both types of allegations, but also something further. Separate from any alleged terrorist activities it stands accused of a different category of transgressions: human rights abuses and "cult"-like behavior.

An organization that serially abuses human rights and brainwashes its subjects into submission, denying their free will and programming them for potentially self-destructive actions, would deserve criticism and perhaps even humanitarian intervention, whether or not these activities were classified as terrorist in nature. State Department officials and government documents have repeatedly cited reports by two respected institutions, the RAND Corporation and Human Rights Watch, attributing such behavior to the MEK. The implication of the most recent references is that the MEK, although now de-listed as an FTO, should still merit the public's moral disdain, and ought not to be treated by the US as a legitimate Iranian political opposition group irrespective of the absence of recent terror activity.

RAND became an important voice on this controversial subject almost inadvertently. During Operation Iraqi Freedom (OIF), the Department of Defense (DoD) was concerned that US forces were responsible for the welfare of as many as 26,000 detainees in Iraq, and tasked RAND to examine the problem. Researchers at RAND focused upon the largest single group—the approximately 3,800 MEK exiles who in 2003 consolidated at Camp Ashraf—and proposed that all of them be returned to Iran, which more than any other single step would lessen the burden on thinly-stretched Military Police units.

RAND's 2009 report[18] fashioned a case that US forces in theater, the Secretary of Defense and DoD lawyers had erred in their legal classification of the MEK by which each individual was granted "protected persons" status under the Fourth Geneva Convention in 2004. The report cited OIF battlefield reporting that, it argued, showed that the MEK had fought against US forces, meriting legal classification as combatants under the Third Geneva Convention, a status affording the US military more latitude.

In making its otherwise copiously documented argument, the RAND report employed a term uncommon in DoD or military parlance:[19] it characterized the MEK as a "cult." Moreover, it used this word not just once, but by one estimate 88 times—surely a record for a publication by a federally-funded national security think tank—and in 2012 the principal author continued to fixate on this aspersion[20] in lieu of defending the report's legal and policy recommendations.

One reason may be that the RAND report's main recommendation—*"several factors suggest that repatriation to Iran is appropriate for the MeK rank and file"*—was gruesomely discredited almost from the moment the report was released, as Iraqi military forces in July 2009 raided Camp Ashraf and opened fire on unarmed men and women. This, the first of two lethal attacks (Figure 7) that together killed 49 and wounded hundreds, was in furtherance of a well-publicized commitment to Iran's Supreme Leader by Iraqi leaders to close Camp Ashraf and evict the MEK.

Tahar Boumedra, Chief Human Rights Officer for the UN Assistance Mission in Iraq beginning in 2009 and the UN official assigned in 2011 to handle matters concerning MEK personnel at Camp Ashraf and Camp Liberty, recently exposed the Iranian Embassy's direct involvement in the Iraqi government's brutal treatment of these exiles. The UN officer who had performed the body count following the second Iraqi assault at Camp Ashraf, in April 2011, Mr. Boumedra attended five meetings at the Iranian Embassy in Baghdad in 2012

Figure 7.
From video of Iraqi HMMWV running over a resident of Camp Ashraf, April 8, 2011. Courtesy, MEK

where Iranian, Iraqi and UN mission officials determined precise dates and numbers for the movements of exiles from Camp Ashraf to Camp Liberty. Iran's *"obvious"* goal, said Mr. Boumedra, is *"to break the exiles' will and morale as an organized group and force their departure."*[21]

The two Iraqi attacks on Camp Ashraf residents, in July 2009 and April 2011, and the subsequent revelations about Iran's intimate collaboration with the office of Iraqi Prime Minister Nouri Al-Maliki in dealing with the MEK presence, offer ample cause to doubt the utility of this report as a guide to the political realities surrounding the MEK exiles in Iraq, notwithstanding RAND's well-established reputation. Yet the US Government nevertheless saw fit to submit it to the Federal Appeals Court as a trusted information resource,[22] and State Department officials continued to reference its description of troubling MEK practices as a basis for assessing the MEK's standing among Iranians.

The report says that many MEK members (p. xvi) *"were victims of … fraudulent recruiting practices"* and that (p. xix), *"JIATF personnel and former MeK members believe that many members of the MeK rank and file would volunteer for repatriation if they were freed of the MeK leadership's authoritarian, cultic practices."* This belief, propagated by RAND as well as a May 2005 Human Rights Watch report[23] which RAND used as a reference, has not been without consequence: it was the basis for the UN Secretariat's (and perhaps the US Government's) endorsement of Iraq's insistence that "refugee status determination" interviews not be conducted at Camp Ashraf.

As the author heard directly from a top UN official in New York in November 2011, the UN Secretariat was convinced that MEK personnel could not speak freely at Camp Ashraf, even though as former UN official Boumedra points out, UNHCR had conducted interviews with Camp Ashraf residents in the past with no issues of coercion or undue leadership influence. Hence, the perceived necessity to establish a new processing facility, and the relocation of the exiles to Camp Liberty.

So certain were foreign diplomats in Iraq that MEK members would seek refuge from their presumed imprisonment once liberated from Camp Ashraf that Baghdad's Al-Muhajir Hotel was reconfigured at no small expense to ensure the security of UN personnel, so that Camp Ashraf residents wishing to return to Iran could be safely housed and debriefed before returning to Iran. Transfers of Camp Ashraf residents to Camp Liberty were staged in increments of approximately 400, in part to ensure their separation from MEK 'leaders' and mitigate against suspected coercive influence.

By the time five transfers totaling 2,000 personnel had gone from Camp Ashraf to Camp Liberty, a completely different reality became clear: not one person asked to go to the Al-Muhajir Hotel or be returned to Iran. The hotel was instead reconfigured to provide for disabled residents coming out of Camp Ashraf in a belated response to international criticism of Camp Liberty's non-compliance with UN humanitarian requirements.[24] Even the disabled chose to remain with their fellow exiles at Camp Liberty, forgoing use of this facility.

Among the RAND researchers' other major errors—leaving aside the spectacle of second-guessing wartime decisions made by commanders in the field backed by cabinet officers and their professional legal staffs in Washington—was to overlook the definitive US Government pronouncement, issued by the Department of State spokesman on July 26, 2004, regarding the question of whether the MEK had fought against US forces in Iraq: "*[W]e have determined that they were not belligerents in this conflict ....*"[25]

Its legal case thus undermined—Fourth Geneva Convention treatment was appropriate after all—and with it a basis for turning this population over to the authorities in Iran, the RAND report's faulty reading of the MEK's circumstances created some reputational risk to the US. The attacks in 2009 and 2011 by Iraqi forces against unarmed men and women in Camp Ashraf, death threats in Farsi amplified almost daily beginning in 2009

Figure 8.
Loudspeakers installed around Camp Ashraf by the Iraqi government to broadcast threatening messages. Courtesy, Camp Ashraf

through loudspeakers arrayed around the site (Figure 8), and other acts of hostility and mistreatment of MEK exiles in Iraq all implicated America's reputation by pointing up the very commitments under international law that the RAND report would have had the US abandon.

The 2004 US decision to accord these people "protected persons" status under the Fourth Geneva Convention was not only prescient in light of the dangers that materialized after US forces withdrew at the end of 2008: it was a formal promise of security made to each individual by the United States. According to former UN official Boumedra, a London-educated expert in international humanitarian law, Article 45 of the Fourth Geneva Convention places continuing responsibility on the United States to see to these people's protection in a case where the *"transferee Power"* (Iraq) *"fails to carry out the provisions of the present Convention in any important respect …."*

One possible reason the RAND report authors were inclined to look for a way around a commitment still embraced by US military officers familiar with the policy was the unsavory portrait of the MEK contained in the Human Rights Watch (HRW) report which RAND cited and to which State Department officials also still refer. HRW reported (p. 1) "*abuses ranging from detention and persecution of ordinary members wishing to leave the organization, to lengthy solitary confinements, severe beatings, and torture of dissident members,*" adding, "*The [MEK] held political dissidents in its internal prisons during the 1990s and later turned over many of them to Iraqi authorities, who held them in Abu Ghraib.*"

A globally esteemed non-governmental organization, HRW alleged that in the mid-1980s, after Massoud and Maryam Rajavi married and presented themselves as the MEK leadership team, they forcibly imposed upon the MEK population abusive measures including (p. 4) *"divorce by decree of married couples, regular writings of self-criticism reports, renunciation of sexuality, and absolute mental and physical dedication to the leadership."* HRW's sources spoke of lengthy detentions, solitary confinement and torture by MEK superiors.

This author has already written (see endnote 4: August 2011 report, Tab 7) about the controversy surrounding HRW's 'research,' consisting of telephonic interviews with 12 individuals residing in Europe. Face-to-face contact was made with these sources (in Europe—HRW representatives never visited Camp Ashraf) only after the fact in an effort to validate the initial report, after a number of these individuals were alleged by MEK members and supporters to be on the payroll or under the influence of Iran's Ministry of Intelligence and Security (MOIS).

A December 2012 report profiling the MOIS by the US Library of Congress's Federal Research Division, prepared for the Pentagon's Combating Terrorism Technical Support Office, describes how the MOIS, during the period 1990–1993, recruited former MEK members and "used them to launch a disinformation campaign against the MEK."[26] One Iranian expatriate living in Europe provided court testimony detailing his prior work as a paid agent of the MOIS, including an assignment specifically supporting *"an extensive campaign to convince Human Rights Watch that PMOI [MEK] is engaged in human rights abuses"* in which the agents *"encouraged them [HRW] to prepare a report in this regard"* (endnote 4, *Op. cit.*).

The MEK was not alone in disputing the HRW allegations. In an extraordinary rebuke, Brigadier General (then-Colonel) David Phillips, at the time the Commander of the 89th Military Police Brigade and responsible for overseeing security at Camp Ashraf throughout 2004, wrote a letter to Kenneth Roth, Executive Director of HRW, on May 27, 2005 in which he called the allegations "an affront to the professionalism" of his units:

> "Over the year-long period I was apprised of numerous reports of torture, of concealed weapons and people being held against their will by the [MEK] leadership …. At no time did we ever discover any credible evidence supporting the allegations raised in your recent report. I would not have tolerated the abuses outlined in your report …. Each report of torture, kidnapping and psychological deprivation turned out to be unsubstantiated …. I believe your recent report was based on unsubstantiated information from individuals without firsthand knowledge or for reasons of personal gain …. I observed a total freedom of choice on the part of the members to either remain or depart from the MEK."[27]

In response to these and other challenges to the report's credibility, including from European Parliamentarians familiar with and supportive of the MEK, the organization released a statement on February 14, 2006 in which it termed the criticisms "unwarranted." HRW did not take issue with the accounts of US military officers with first-hand knowledge of Camp Ashraf and its population from 2003 on. Rather, it clarified that its 2005 report pertained only to conditions within Camp Ashraf *"from 1991 until February 2003."*

Figure 11. Trailers at Camp Liberty after residents relocated from Camp Ashraf. Courtesy, Camp Liberty

Figure 9. (top) Library in Camp Ashraf.
Figure 10. (bottom) Cultural performance, Camp Ashraf. Courtesy, Camp Ashraf

Even during the decade-plus during which HRW says these abusive conditions existed, available evidence does not support the allegations. The International Committee of the Red Cross (ICRC) in Baghdad reported in September 1992 that it had interviewed 591 "former Iranian POWs or Iranian servicemen" resident with the MEK in Iraq. It said: *"During the visit, the ICRC Delegation could interview without witness the 591 Iranian nationals in order to establish their identity and to ascertain whether or not they wished to be repatriated to their country of origin. None of the 591 persons met during the visit wished to be repatriated."* The statement continued, *"[T]he ICRC no longer considers the 591 former POWs as protected persons under the Geneva Conventions of 1949, and will therefore not visit them again."*[28]

That such allegations, whether fact or fabrication, are not alleged by HRW to have occurred during the past decade seems not to have deterred the RAND report authors or US officials years later from associating the MEK with extreme human rights abuses against its own people. It is ironic that officials today would tout a report featuring allegations of *"solitary confinement inside a small pre-fabricated trailer room ('bangal')*," as over 3,000 MEK residents were, with high-level US encouragement, relocated in 2012 from well-provisioned facilities at Camp Ashraf (Figures 9, 10) to an austere, 0.6 square kilometer internment facility with virtually nowhere for them to go except inside their 'small, prefabricated trailer rooms' (Figure 11).

Questionable though sources may have been for information on alleged past MEK abusive practices, the reality is that such derogatory characterizations routinely appear today in news stories and commentaries on the MEK. As with the terror allegations, closer consideration of the circumstances surrounding the organization may shed light on the nature of MEK life in Iraq.

The fortunes of the group seem to have declined after the end of the Iran-Iraq war in the late 1980s. Many MEK members and supporters in Iranian jails were executed *en masse* (details below). The MEK's military arm, the NLA, suffered heavy losses during an ambitious military incursion into Iran days after Ayatollah Khomeini announced a cease-fire in the war, and pulled back into Iraq, never again to mount another large-scale operation. The clerical government in Iran successfully managed its leadership succession, confirming the new Supreme Leader Ali Khamenei following the death of Ayatollah Khomeini.

The security of the MEK population at Camp Ashraf deteriorated after Saddam Hussein's forces invaded Kuwait in August 1990, as Coalition warplanes targeted sites throughout southern Iraq during the Gulf War, 14 of 18 Iraqi provinces revolted against the Baghdad regime and were brutally subjugated in the spring of 1991, and Iranian warplanes bombed Camp Ashraf in April 1992. MEK sources say members were attacked and killed by elite Iranian "Quds Force" agents in Iraq, citing well over 100 attacks against MEK personnel and property from 1993 to 2003. Having shuttled children out through Jordan to friends and relatives in other countries during Operation Desert Storm to ensure their survival, the remaining MEK consolidated within Camp Ashraf and a few other bases, unsure that residence inside Iraq would any longer afford them sanctuary.

Under such duress, the MEK population in Iraq appears to have intensified its focus on the organization's structure, purposes and beliefs. It may indeed have become more regimented in culture and austere in lifestyle, more psychologically dependent upon its leaders, and more engaged in training and doctrinal study. The comparison is apt to an isolated military outpost in a dangerous locale, where the people serve 'unaccompanied' tours and fraternization is deemed detrimental to the mission. These factors, with the unique added feature of Muslim women in leadership roles, have struck some Western observers as bizarre.

The importance to the MEK of its embrace of gender equality as a direct reproach of what the group terms "religious fascism" in Iran should not be underestimated. Maryam Rajavi has lectured often on this subject,[29] saying, *"The essential characteristic of the fundamentalism ruling Iran is its misogynist nature"*; from her perspective, *"just as Hitler's Nazi ideology was based on racial supremacy, Khomeini's fundamentalist culture and ideology are based on gender apartheid and sexual discrimination."* She cites a *"century-long struggle for equality"* by Iranian women, dating to the 1906 constitutional uprising in which Iran first created a Parliament. Mrs. Rajavi highlights the role of women in that movement, which *"led to the establishment, for the first time, of girls' schools and introduction of women's education"* as well as the formation of women's societies and the first woman's journal.

From the time the MEK founders' views were first disseminated, the MEK's university student supporters included many women; and women, including girls, have not been spared the full brunt of regime punishments for presumed pro-MEK views. When in 1989 Mrs. Rajavi was elected to the position of MEK Secretary General, she instituted changes that would accord women an equal say in MEK decisionmaking, reflecting the equal measure of hardship they had endured.

With the MEK having been discussed in US policy circles for the past 15 years solely in connection with its status as a listed terrorist organization, one will not find much American awareness of the group's commitment to gender equality; however, its significance has not gone unnoticed elsewhere. On June 23, 2012, Ingrid Betancourt, the former Senator and Presidential candidate in Colombia who survived over six years as a FARC hostage and was rescued in 2008, said this while addressing Mrs. Rajavi at a MEK rally near Paris:

> "I have a special message for the women of Ashraf [now Camp Liberty], my sisters. I want to tell them that I'm very proud to be on the same side fighting this combat with Maryam Rajavi. Don't you think it's … a nice happening in the history of the world that this group of criminals that are misogynists, that have enacted those laws against women in Iran, are going to be defeated by a woman? Don't you think this is great? …. I believe strongly in God. And I think that … God has humor, and He knows how to prove that He is the one ruling. And so that's why Maryam is going to be the next president in free Iran."

Male MEK members have told the author of their initial mixed feelings and difficulty in adjusting when Massoud and Maryam Rajavi first advanced the notion of fully empowering the women in their ranks in the late 1980s, including as commanding 'officers' in their military wing. By contrast, today this step as much as any other is heralded within the MEK by both sexes as one of its proudest achievements. But at the time, the future significance of such steps was not on the minds of the exiles in Iraq, most of whom made the decision, as Mrs. Rajavi has put it, *"to forsake family life and concentrate all energies, power, affections and attention to the struggle against the religious fascism for the cause of freedom and equality in Iran."*

Accordingly, some may have decided not to accept such a level of personal commitment; others may have lost interest and left the MEK once the costly 1988 incursion spelled the end of major military operations. It seems to have been a time that tested each individual's willingness to set aside other life priorities to continue a long and uncertain struggle to effect regime change in Tehran. Life at these bases near the Iran border, in sum, was probably unappealing for some, fulfilling for others, and in any case far removed from quotidien life on the outside.

Before concluding that the above conditions merit a disparaging description such as "cult," one ought to measure life inside Iran against an equivalent standard. There, the regime demands total fealty and harshly enforces social and religious obeisance while exercising political control at gunpoint, as it were, all in the name of Islam. As troubling as the alleged MEK abuses are, they are not of comparable severity and scope to known abuses by the regime in Iran. Iranian intelligence has repeatedly been caught disseminating unattributed allegations abroad of MEK human rights abuses and 'cult-like' behavior. One might reasonably question on what basis officials, journalists and policy commentators in the West continue to give credence to charges of such suspect credibility that even HRW does not allege beyond 2003.

Nevertheless, UN and US officials apparently believed that the prospect of coercion by MEK 'leaders' over the rank and file inside Camp Ashraf merited extraordinary measures during the past year before MEK exiles in Iraq could be properly interviewed as potential refugees. The MEK did the one thing it could do to prove its readiness to forego any such 'coercive powers': it vacated Camp Ashraf and gave the UN control over the future disposition of the MEK population, accepting the prospect of permanent dispersal of these people to willing countries anywhere. As for the UN and US, it is hard to see how their professed concern about coercive leadership influence over individuals to be processed by UNHCR was ameliorated by herding over 3,000 men and women, leaders and all, into a locked-down trailer park one-seventieth the size of Camp Ashraf.

The Survivors' Burden

Suppose, for the sake of argument, that all of the allegations against the MEK are true, and that the public dossier is a reliable chronicle of its past activities. When the public sees a member of the now-de-listed MEK, can they assume they are looking at a genuine ex-terrorist?

The State Department *Country Reports* estimates the total MEK population worldwide at 5,000–10,000, with many in Europe. Of the roughly 3,200 still in Iraq, the RAND report estimated (p. 49) that *"approximately 70 percent ... joined the MEK after the group relocated to Iraq."* That means that well over 2,000 of the MEK members resident in Iraq from the early 1980s on had no hand in any of the alleged MEK acts of violence inside Iran after the regime declared war on the MEK in mid-1981; nor can these people be connected to any alleged MEK acts of violence or a role in the Embassy seizure during the 1970s. While numerical estimates are obviously imprecise, the point is that not all MEK members are of the same generation or began their involvement at the same time.

Recall that in 2004, every resident of Camp Ashraf was privately interviewed by the Department of State, and then individually investigated by a US interagency team representing the Department of Justice, FBI, Defense Intelligence Agency, CIA, Immigration and Naturalization Service, military intelligence and Department of Homeland Security. No charges were brought by US authorities against anyone. As for the Europe-based part of the organization, the top 160 MEK members arrested on terror charges in France in 2003 were investigated by the courts—some for eight years—and, as noted, fully exonerated in 2011.

Not only must a rigorous review of the MEK dossier conclude that much of what has long been accepted as fact about its alleged activities is untrue. It must now be admitted as well that the US and European authorities—all four of whose "terrorist" classifications of the MEK have now been reinvestigated and undone—have failed to convict a single person considered to be a MEK member of any prosecutable act.

Figure 12. ▶
Two MEK members hung from a railway bridge in southern Iran in mid-1981. Courtesy MEK

One individual who is being pursued for violent crimes, by the Spanish judiciary, is the Iraqi officer in charge of security at Camp Liberty. Colonel Sadiq Mohammed Kazem led the Iraqi military unit that massacred defenseless MEK residents at Camp Ashraf in April 2011—an attack which, along with the July 2009 attack by Iraqi forces, left 49 killed and several hundred wounded. Colonel Sadiq would be banned under US law from ever receiving US military training due to his history as a gross violator of human rights. He was refused entry to the European Parliament while accompanying an Iraqi delegation in June 2012 and detained by French police before being sent home. Why the UN and the US consumed a year of diplomatic effort to remove the MEK population from Camp Ashraf only to place it under this officer's 'protection' has yet to be explained.

As problematical as it may be to tie current MEK members to past alleged terrorist activities, there is one link to the past shared by MEK members of every generation: the loss of one or more family members at the hands of Iranian security forces. To match even the State Department's maximum estimate of 10,000 MEK members to the lowest estimates of MEK members known to have been executed or otherwise killed by the Shah's or the clerical regime's enforcers is to contemplate a killed-to-survivors ratio well in excess of 2:1. Using a median figure of 7,500 MEK members and credible casualty estimates, that ratio could be five or ten to one. To be introduced to a member of the MEK is, more often than not, to learn about members of his or her family whose lives were taken by the state, often at a young age.

These people have suffered immense personal losses over the last forty years—as many as 120,000 members and suspected sympathizers dead, according to MEK sources. In the past century, war and famine have produced large death tolls, as has genocide based on religion or ethnicity. Yet there are few if any modern parallels to the state-administered executions by Iran's clerics of MEK members and suspected sympathizers in an effort to extinguish public attraction to their beliefs (Figure 12).

Here the evidence is strong, as families have preserved the memories of their lost loved ones. As harsh as the Shah's SAVAK secret police and military courts were in dealing with the MEK from 1971–79, the clerical regime since 1979 has been orders of magnitude more brutal. The prisons under Ayatollah Khomeini witnessed mass executions of MEK members and many suspected of helping or harboring sympathy for the MEK, including

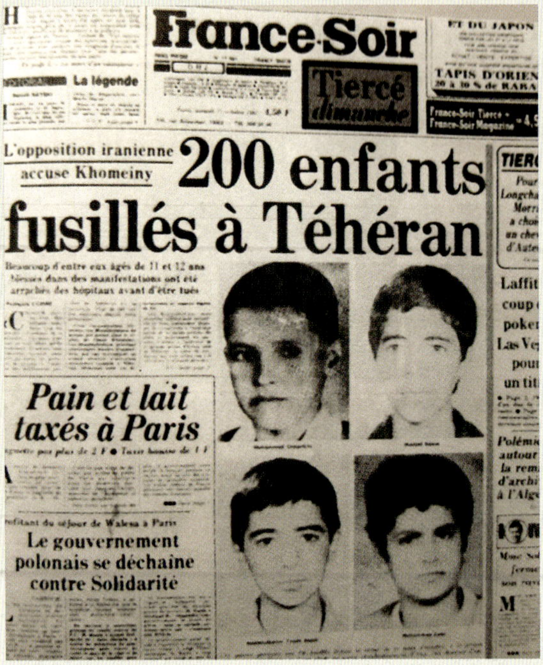
France-Soir

Tiercé dimanche

La légende

ET DU JAPON

TAPIS D'ORIENT

L'opposition iranienne accuse Khomeiny

200 enfants fusillés à Téhéran

Beaucoup d'entre eux âgés de 11 et 12 ans blessés dans des manifestations ont été arrachés des hôpitaux avant d'être tués

Pain et lait taxés à Paris

Le gouvernement polonais se déchaîne contre Solidarité

Figure 13.
France-Soir, reporting on the execution of children during the regime's 'reign of terror' beginning in 1981. Courtesy, MEK

children (Figure 13). The clerics' security forces raided and bombed MEK members in their homes and offices, shot them in the streets, and assassinated key members abroad. Iranian regime forces attacked MEK camps in Iraq with aerial bombardment in 1992 as noted, and with dozens of SCUD missiles in 2001.

The admiration evident throughout the MEK for the organization's leaders, Massoud and Maryam Rajavi, which Western critics interpret as cult-like devotion, is less difficult to comprehend when one considers their personal histories.

Massoud Rajavi's wife Ashraf was gunned down in Tehran on February 8, 1982 after he had sought refuge in France from the wave of regime attacks. His only sister, Monireh, was executed along with her husband in 1988. His brother Professor Kazem Rajavi, who had served as Iran's post-revolutionary Ambassador to the UN in Geneva, was assassinated by regime agents in Geneva on April 24, 1990. Maryam Rajavi's sister Narges was executed by the security services during the Shah's reign. Another sister Massoumeh was tortured to death in jail by the clerical regime despite being eight months pregnant at the time. Mrs. Rajavi has a son, 32, and a daughter, 30, among the MEK population recently transferred from Camp Ashraf to Camp Liberty.

Their stories are not unique.

Geoffrey Robertson, a widely-published British human rights lawyer and Professor in Human Rights Law at Queen Mary College who served as President and Appeal Judge for the UN War Crimes Court in Sierra Leone, conducted an independent inquiry[30] in 2009 of the suspected massacre in 1988 of MEK political prisoners at Ayatollah Khomeini's direction. A UN Special Representative assigned to Iran at the time, Robertson found, had heard reports of mass executions but encountered *"complete denial"* from the regime, which dismissed his information as *"unreliable [MEK] propaganda."*

Over two decades later, reviewing extensive documentation from the period, Professor Robertson provided an account of what had actually transpired beginning in July 1988. Prisons filled with suspected MEK sympathizers—some close to completing their jail sentences—were subjected to a sudden halt in all activities and family contacts, and each prisoner was briefly visited by a regime "delegation" consisting of a religious judge, a public prosecutor and an intelligence official. As Robertson writes (p. 1):

> "The delegation had but one question for these young men and women (most of them detained since 1981 merely for taking part in street protests or possession of 'political' reading material), and although they did not know it, on the answer their life would depend. Those who by that answer evinced any continuing affiliation with the *Mojahedin* were blindfolded and ordered to join a conga-line that led straight to the gallows. They were hung from cranes, four at a time, or in groups of six from ropes hanging from the front of the stage in an assembly hall; some were taken to army barracks at night … and then shot by firing squad. Their bodies were doused with disinfectant, packed in refrigerated trucks and buried by night in mass graves. Months later their families … would be handed a plastic bag with their few possessions. They would be refused any information about the location of the graves and ordered never to mourn them in public. By mid-August 1988, thousands of prisoners had been killed in this manner by the state …."

Khomeini had issued a *fatwa* requiring death for all who adhere to the MEK's beliefs. When such a sweeping decree was challenged by colleagues, says Robertson, Khomeini's response (p. 7) was, *"[T]he sentence is execution for everyone who at any stage or at any time maintains his or her support for the Monafeqin [MEK] organisation."* Robertson's conclusion (p. 98) is that the definition accepted today of Crimes Against Humanity, based on the Rome Statute, *"would plainly cover the extermination of the [MEK]."*

Thanks to the memoir, published by his students and religious protégés, of one very senior cleric, Grand Ayatollah Hossein Ali Montazeri, there is an explicit record of Montazeri's 1988 correspondence with Supreme Leader Khomeini in which Montazeri repeatedly questioned the propriety of summarily executing people who were serving lighter sentences, some nearing completion.[31] Montazeri's moral objections irritated Khomeini and led him to remove Montazeri—a Shi'ite *Grand Marja* and Iran's most respected Islamic scholar—as his designated successor to become Supreme Leader.

This opened the way for Khomeini's more dependable lieutenant Ali Khamenei to assume the holy authority of the 12th Imam. Although Khamenei had inferior religious credentials—both his *Ayatollah* and *Grand Ayatollah* religious 'ranks' had to be conferred by party vote, not unlike Saddam Hussein's military rank of Field Marshal in Iraq—he could be counted on to remember always that his prime duty was regime preservation.

Reporting in 1990, even before the full extent of the executions had come to light, Amnesty International wrote of *"a government policy which is apparently intoxicated with the death penalty as a catch-all solution …. In some quarters in Iran the death penalty seems to have the status of a virtue in itself …."*[32] (The MEK's political affiliate, the National Council of Resistance of Iran, has adopted a policy that would abolish the death penalty in Iran.)

MEK sources today speak of procedures used at the notorious Evin Prison in 1988 to kill over 50 persons at a time; of hand grenades thrown into prisoners' cells; and use of swimming pools to facilitate the draining of blood from executed prisoners. Professor Robertson reported (p. 81) that Asadollah Lajevardi, the notorious prison warden known as the "Butcher of Evin" who became head of Iran's Prisons Organization in 1989, was *"said to have forced [MEK] virgins to 'marry' Revolutionary Guards so that they could be raped in order to resolve theological difficulties that stand in the way of executing virgins."*

Just as the court in France investigating the MEK's record in recent years posed the question of whether violence can ever be justified (in the MEK's case it answered affirmatively), the violence by Iran's leadership against its political opponents, which Western governments have generally filed under the rubric of counterterrorism, demands reassessment. Tehran has sought to conceal this kind of information, and much may still be unknown to the outside world. President Khatami, whose moderation was to have been the reward for America's initial listing of the MEK as a FTO in 1997, personally ordered the closure of the *Arya* daily, and the Ministry of Guidance enforced the closure according to the daily *Gozaresh* on April 9, 2000, after *"[Arya] carried a story about the massacre of political prisoners in 1988."*

A number of American policy analysts who dismiss the MEK's potential ever to gain public acceptance in Iran are admirers of Mir Hussein Moussavi, leader of the so-called "Green Movement." This popular movement arose to challenge incumbent Mahmoud Ahmadinejad during Iran's 2009 Presidential elections, which were marred by widely reported irregularities and street demonstrations that were put down with excessive force by police. Moussavi remains under house arrest, a politician with stature who embodies the hopes of many in the West for reform in Iran. He also remains under review by international legal experts for possible complicity in crimes against humanity in 1988, when he was Iran's Prime Minister during the mass extermination of MEK members and supporters, which was immediately followed by a wave of executions of secular leftists.

The 1988 mass killings of political prisoners in Iran were *"of greater infamy,"* concluded Robertson's inquiry, than the Japanese death marches of World War II or the 1995 massacre at Srebrenica in Bosnia-Herzegovina.

Recapitulating an earlier theme, this entire saga is a conflict between two parties. Knowing of the heinous atrocities and massive death toll systematically inflicted on MEK individuals, families and suspected sympathizers by the Iranian state over the past three decades, if one had been told by the US Government only of violent actions by the MEK (e.g., 2011 *Country Reports:* "*The MEK … assassinated the former Iranian Minister of Prisons [Lajevardi] in 1998.*"), one might justifiably ponder whether the intent was to inform the public or mislead it.

For the US: Lessons Learned—Liabilities and Remedies

From the foregoing review it will be clear that the US Government's publicly shared information about the MEK and its activities has changed, materially and dramatically, over the years, in a direction further from rather than closer to the truth. The official MEK dossier today is tainted with demonstrable errors of fact, allegations of highly dubious provenance, and seriously misleading accounts of fateful historical events—distortions that go beyond the mild excesses of bureaucrats eager to put the strongest 'case' for a terrorist designation in front of higher officials, Congress and the public.

Long gone is the Department of State's view, in a December 1984 memorandum to Congress, that *"Mujahedin ideology is a major source of the group's popularity in Iran. It has been crafted with care and applied with consistency to both domestic and foreign issues—often in great detail …. The Mujahedin present their program … as a dynamic response to the problems of modern Iran …"* Gone as well is the memo's description of the MEK's founders as *"disaffected young members of the Liberation Movement of Iran, which … initially advocated the use of peaceful means to create a new regime that combined a constitutional monarchy with Western European-style socialism;"* or its goal of *"providing a popular voice in all aspects of national life through 'a truly democratic power structure',"* reflected in its actions after the 1979 revolution when it *"unsuccessfully sought a freely-elected constituent assembly to draft a constitution."*[33]

Long forgotten is the inaugural 1993 *Patterns of Global Terrorism*'s description of the MEK: *"Formed in the 1960's by the college-educated children of Iranian merchants, the MEK sought to counter what is perceived as excessive Western influence in the Shah's regime. In the 1970s, the MEK—led by Masud Rajavi after 1978—concluded that violence was the only way to bring about change in Iran. … The MEK directs a worldwide campaign against the Iranian Government that stresses propaganda and occasionally uses terrorist violence. … Since the mid-1980s, the MEK has not mounted terrorist operations into Iran at a level similar to its activities in the 1970s. Aside from the National Liberation Army's attacks into Iran toward the end of the Iran-Iraq war, and occasional NLA cross-border incursions since, the MEK's attacks on Iran have amounted to little more than harassment. The MEK has had more success in confronting Iranian representatives overseas through propaganda and street demonstrations."*

In the 19 years since those words were approved for publication by offices throughout the US national security bureaucracy, different words have entered the government's narrative. Some have added clarity such as the 2005 *Country Reports'* explanation that it had been a breakaway splinter group that killed Americans in Iran during the 1970s, although that crucial exculpatory information vanished without explanation in later editions. More often, material and prose have been added or revised with no other apparent purpose than to pad the indictment against the MEK. Starting with the 2006 *Reports* when a raft of new and sensational depictions of past events appeared, and again with the 2009 *Reports* when events decades earlier that had been minimized or dropped from previous annual editions resurfaced with new implied significance, the file has been embellished.

Is there new intelligence proving that the MEK was always more hostile to democratic ideals than originally thought? Or that its violent acts caused far more severe harm than was noticed at the time? With successive tellings, the account of MEK activities going back to the early 1970s has acquired new attributes that speak more to the MEK members' supposedly deplorable nature than to the group's alleged crimes, as if to suggest that the group and its supporters deserve our opprobrium regardless of the particulars. That officials have seen fit to highlight reports depicting malignant social and cultural conditions within MEK camps—even were these accounts supported by more credible information—raises further questions, as this topic contributes nothing to the task of proving or disproving the group's responsibility for acts of terrorism threatening US interests.

The MEK's case has implications for how the US Government assesses terror threats. There are clearly issues of validating facts before they are released to the public as official information, not to mention relied upon as a basis for policy. There could also be grounds for concern about undue influence of individuals involved in the process with undeclared biases or agendas shaped by familial ties in countries to be affected by US policy. There is, finally, the lingering question of how little or how much factual justification is enough to sustain a FTO designation if US policymakers have foreign policy reasons for wishing to list an entity.

Three active initiatives should follow the de-listing of the MEK.

First, the MEK's extensive intelligence network and archives should be fully accessed by US agencies. This is not to be confused with operational collaboration or political support. The MEK has, for personal survival reasons if no other, been keeping closer tabs than anyone on the mullahs' and their security branches' activities both inside and outside Iran for many years. European experts including the former head of a national counterterrorism service are familiar with and laudatory of the MEK's intelligence capabilities, which were credited by US leaders with having revealed Iran's illicit nuclear activities a decade ago. At a time when US-Iran tensions continue to escalate toward possible conflict, there is no good reason why the US should not avail itself of—and, of course, evaluate for itself—all available information on Iran, including from the MEK.

Second, the US should undertake a thorough counterintelligence review given that the MEK dossier has been so extensively manipulated. People who are fond of drawing alarmist comparisons between the MEK and the Iraqi exiles who misled the US in securing its support prior to the 2003 Iraq intervention are right in one respect: US intelligence was faulty in both instances. Iran's Ministry of Intelligence and Security has demonstrated a focus different from other major foreign intelligence services: it has been less interested in obtaining military and technological secrets, and more interested in persuading foreign capitals to enlist their own instruments of enforcement in the service of Tehran's war against its critics abroad. The MOIS' use of agents to spread derogatory information on the MEK in several countries has repeatedly been exposed. Is anyone in Washington prepared to say there are no such MOIS activities aimed at shaping US policies?

Third, the US would be well served by paying more attention to the political dimension of Iran's domestic and international situation, the better to understand potential leverage points on Iran's leadership as the current crisis develops. At almost any Washington think tank discussion on Iran today, one will hear policy experts talk about numbers of centrifuges, quantities of uranium and levels of enrichment, probability of success of an air strike and—the most discussed topic—estimated times before Iran's nuclear program reaches key thresholds of capability. Americans are, of course, right to focus on this, the most urgent and consequential danger posed by Iran. But the nuclear challenge presented by Iran's leadership conveniently diverts and even monopolizes foreign attention. The ruling clerics have been getting a free pass from the US on their legitimacy problems at home, including suppression of the people's democratic aspirations; judicial excesses; lack of transparency on the use of national revenues for their favored institutions and activities; fomenting of violence, terror and corruption abroad; and erosion of public regard for the way they have carried out their politically sacrosanct "guardianship" role in the name of Islam.

With Iran representing a major threat to US interests, there is precious little discussion about the men who run it, and the motivations behind their actions. The Iranian regime has been using a variety of means to advance its interests, and has capitalized on opportunities within its neighborhood to add to America's burdens. During the US and Coalition intervention in Iraq, two Arabic language stations based in Iran broadcast into Iraq, heavily promoting the theme that the US was undermining Iraqi sovereignty when, for example, American officials were seeking to negotiate a stay-behind military presence in Iraq beyond 2008—ultimately without success.

Deadly Iranian weapons including shaped-charge Improvised Explosive Devices and Man-Portable Air Defense Systems turned up in Iraq, used against US and Coalition forces. More recently, as the *New York Times* reported on April 4, 2012, *"Just hours after it was revealed that American soldiers had burned Korans seized at an Afghan detention center in late February, Iran secretly ordered its agents operating inside Afghanistan to exploit the anticipated public outrage by trying to instigate violent protests in the capital, Kabul, and across the western part of the country …."* Thirty died in these protests, including four Americans.

Iran has reportedly maintained a weapons supply[34] and has acknowledged sending elite forces[35] to support the Syrian regime; it has for years been *"funneling rifle and machine-gun ammunition into regions of protracted conflict"* in Africa, eluding detection;[36] long-range rockets supplied by Iran to Hamas have *"significantly increased the danger to Israel's major cities"*;[37] and Yemeni authorities have intercepted weapons being smuggled from *"an Iranian military-controlled port"* including Chinese and Russian model shoulder-fired anti-aircraft missiles, explosives, machine-gun ammunition, night vision goggles and laser range-finders, believed to be intended for Shi'ite insurgents in Yemen.[38]

In the media domain, having closed down Iran's leading film directors union in 2012, the authorities have set up *"several foreign language channels to spread their ideology"* and are now producing a major film depicting the regime's view of the 1979 hostage crisis.[39] Iranian diplomats, meanwhile, portray their country as the aggrieved party in its international dealings, ever deflecting attention from a focused reckoning of Iran's serial violations of international norms and commitments, including major terrorist acts in which some among its current leadership played significant roles.[40]

These examples of destabilizing arms transfers, psychological operations and regime propaganda illustrate Tehran's propensity to pursue activities more likely to achieve significant effects at a low cost, impacting US security interests on many fronts but often surreptitiously, without provoking US retaliation. Costly and labor-intensive assistance efforts by the US, several other governments and the UN aimed at stabilizing conflict-prone areas are being directly undermined by Iran's promiscuous arming and proselytizing of extremist non-state actors far from its own borders. At the same time, assassins from Iran's Intelligence Ministry have killed regime opponents of all persuasions in Baghdad, Berlin, Dubai, Geneva, Istanbul, Karachi, Oslo, Paris, Rome and Stockholm,[41] not to mention the foiled plan to target the Saudi Ambassador on US soil.

To contemplate the thirty-year conflict between the ruling mullahs and the MEK is to recognize that as much as the regime may wish to avoid tougher sanctions and air strikes against its nuclear facilities, it is actively subverting US security objectives on many fronts and has waged nothing short of an all-out effort at home and abroad, including resort to mass murder, to silence criticism from those Iranians who understand them best. The time to assess whether there are more effective pressure points on Tehran than economic sanctions is before, not after, a regional nuclear arms race becomes irreversible.

And should the pressures on the clerical regime ever signal the possibility that Iran's 79 million citizens may, at long last, be able to participate meaningfully in their own governance, US officials will want to reacquaint themselves with the past century of thwarted democratic movements in Iran and America's regrettably prominent place on the wrong side of that history.

For the MEK: What Now?

Having protested its classification as a terrorist group for so long, the MEK will doubtless recalibrate its focus onto other objectives now that it has been de-listed in Washington. The near-term priority will be assuring adequate living conditions and securing safe passage out of Iraq for the population still at risk[42] inside Camp Liberty. A pre-dawn rocket attack on February 9, 2013 against MEK residents sleeping in their trailers killed seven and seriously wounded many others. Occurring within a heavily-guarded Iraqi military zone, this precise assault with approximately 36 rockets fired at short range was, in the words of Scottish

Member of the European Parliament (and MEK supporter) Struan Stevenson, "as inevitable as it was preventable."[43]

UNHCR can expect pressure to accelerate refugee processing, and Western governments will hear appeals to accept all of the exiles, made more urgent by the threat communicated to the Associated Press on February 26 by the head of Iraq's Hezbollah Brigades, a group claiming support including weapons from Iran, to continue to "strike" the MEK "until they leave [Iraq]."[44]

Beyond this humanitarian concern, the NCRI will likely endeavor to increase its support and favorable visibility in the US. It will not be an easy task. Experts who have long based their analysis upon the familiar litany of historical MEK information will be loath to revise their positions despite the revelation of how thoroughly the dossier has been corrupted. Leading journalists whose livelihoods benefit from receipt of visas to travel to Iran will continue to steer clear of what is, to put it mildly, a sensitive issue for the regime.

One widespread opinion inside the Washington Beltway that may prove particularly resistant to change is that the MEK is not seen as *"a viable opposition or democratic opposition movement"* or *"an organization that could promote the democratic values that we would like to see in Iran,"* as a senior State Department official put it on September 28, 2012 when backgrounding the press on the de-listing. Among the many analysts following Iranian affairs in Washington, the common view is that the MEK does not enjoy support inside Iran.

Their usual explanation includes the belief that most Iranians regard MEK members as traitors for having 'sided' with Saddam Hussein against their own country during the 8-year Iran-Iraq war. There is no question that the MEK was a welcome guest of Saddam Hussein, basing its activities inside Iraq beginning in the early 1980s; that its military wing (the NLA) obtained significant military equipment from the Iraqi regime (although the MEK says it paid Iraq for all weapons and other goods provided to the group); and that the NLA staged major operations into Iran from bases in Iraq during this time.

MEK supporters challenge the prevailing interpretation. They say many MEK members inside Iran went to the front in late 1980 to defend Iran after the Iraqi incursion, but the clerical regime's forces turned them back. This claim is supported by the aforementioned 1984 State Department memo to Congress which said (pp. 9–10) that when Iraq invaded Iran,

"Mujahedin units went to the front immediately. They were tolerated by the fundamentalists only in the first hectic days of the war, and most were soon expelled."

Supporters also say that the MEK never fought on Iraq's side[45] against Iran, and that only after Iran had regained all of its territory from Iraq in June of 1982 did Massoud Rajavi try repeatedly to broker an equitable cease-fire arrangement including exchange of POWs. In their view, Khomeini unnecessarily perpetuated the conflict for six more years, at ruinous cost to Iran's economy and to Iranian conscripts who suffered casualties, solely as a means to consolidate the regime's control at home and divert resources to its own use. By some estimates, upwards of 90 percent of Iran's war-related deaths occurred after it had regained control of its territory. To have opposed the regime's destructive war policy once Iraq's forces had been expelled was, in the MEK view, a patriotic stance.

Regardless of such explanations, the MEK will be hard-pressed to undo ingrained perceptions as it seeks to build its political campaign against the clerical regime. Defending its patriotism despite years of being hosted by Iran's wartime enemy would be difficult enough in a free society; the Iranian population, however, has lived for over 30 years inside an environment where television, radio, newspapers and most Internet content have carried only regime-approved material. Even though popular disapproval of Khomeini's perpetuation of the war with Iraq may run deep within Iran, the people have heard the MEK referred to only in the most vituperative terms since 1980–81 when the mullahs consolidated control.

For their part, western publics have, as a consequence of the MEK's various national terror listings, frequently heard that the MEK's funding was primarily supplied by Saddam Hussein and otherwise illicitly funneled through front organizations in contravention of government sanctions. The language of law enforcement has framed the MEK's public story in the West for years. Neither inside nor outside of Iran has the MEK been portrayed in the media as a group with significant popular support or legitimately-obtained resources.

Now freed from the restrictions and stigma of FTO designation, the MEK's members and supporters will have the opportunity to contest not only the factual record but assessments dismissive of the group's political potential. Their first and obvious point will be that no one knows how Iranians would vote in a free and open election.

Less obvious to outsiders, apparently—since analysts sometimes note the lack of visible support for the MEK on the Iranian 'street'—is the paramount effect of the Islamic

Punishment Act in Iran. Anyone who is a *"supporter"* of the MEK or *"in any way active or effective in advancing the cause"* of the MEK is guilty of *"waging war on God"* (Article 186), requiring one of four punishments (Article 190) to be selected by a religious judge:

   a. Execution;
   b. Hanging;
   c. Amputation of right arm followed by amputation of left leg;
   d. Banishment or exile.

A UN Human Rights Council special investigator reported in March 2012 that Iran had executed 670 people in 2011, 249 of them secretly.[46] Demonstrations in Iran in February 2011, inspired by the public uprisings then ongoing in Tunisia and Egypt, had the Tehran authorities blaming *"hypocrites, monarchists, ruffians and seditionists"* according to *Fars* news agency, the first of these epithets being the favored regime term for the MEK. Most of those arrested and executed following the June 2009 post-election protests were MEK members, and the authorities blamed the MEK for leading the protests on December 27 of that year coinciding with the holy day of *Ashura*. This is amply documented in the Iranian press over the ensuing months, covering arrests and trials of people described as members of this "terrorist grouplet," "hypocrites," and an "armed anti-Iran organization," most charged with "waging war on God."[47]

An aide to the Supreme Leader in early 2012 falsely blamed the MEK for the assassinations of Iranian nuclear scientists (an allegation the State Department refuted, but only several months after NBC News had reported confirmation of the MEK's role by "two senior US officials").[48] In October 2012, the regime blamed the MEK for unrest over the sharp decline in the value of the rial, Iran's currency.

Regardless of what foreign policy analysts may claim, the regime itself is treating the MEK as a factor inside the country, continuously disparaging the group in an apparent effort to manage public opinion. The aforementioned December 2012 Library of Congress study (endnote 26) states, *"The Iranian government and its intelligence apparatus consider the MEK the most serious dissident organization with regard to the Revolution"*—this even though, as the US Government has now formally acknowledged, the MEK's activities for the past decade have been entirely political and non-violent.

Figure 14.
Satirical skit broadcast on Iran National Television. Courtesy, IRANNTV

The exiled resistance is not ceding the information realm to the clerics. From studios in Europe, Iran National Television (IRANNTV) generates Farsi language programming with news, entertainment and political satire (Figure 14) that is broadcast over leased French and American commercial satellites into Iran and other geographies to reach the diaspora.

To block the transmission signal, the Iranian government has deployed infrared (IR) jammers in Tehran (Figures 15, 16), and the network runs instruction videos on how to shield rooftop satellite dishes from IR interference (Figure 17).

In their search for answers to the question of where the exiled resistance has been getting its money, US Treasury investigators have surely seen the broadcast telethons on IRANNTV, held 3–4 times a year (Figure 18). One such event in July 2011, planned for two days, ran for six days as 23 telephone lines were saturated for 64 hours with calls from Europe, Australia, North America, the Caucasus, India and, Iran, and raised $3.28 million according to the network. More recently, the IRANNTV telethon beginning January 26, 2013 ran for four days, reportedly raising a record $4.13 million with an unprecedented number of calls coming from Iran.

Some of those calling from inside Iran—many of whom the network says waited hours for an open line as the regime sought to disrupt outgoing telephony—would pledge very modest amounts of money collected from family members and friends, risking arrest and even death[49] for the opportunity to address the pro-resistance global audience and offer support.

The day after the June 23, 2012 NCRI rally near Paris, attended by political figures and notables from 31 countries who addressed an estimated 100,000 supporters inside and

Figures 15, 16 and inset.
Iranian regime signal jamming devices arrayed high above Tehran on Milad Tower. Courtesy, IRANNTV and MEK

Figure 17.
Courtesy, IRANNTV

Figure 18.
Courtesy, IRANNTV

outside the exposition hall, the author spoke with a veteran MEK member. Far from evasive on the topic of funding sources for the resistance, he was defiant: *"They say our money came from Saddam Hussein. He has been gone for nine years. How much did that rally cost yesterday? Millions. They owe us an apology."*

What is likely to surprise American observers most about this group, its having just been removed from the terrorism list, is its demeanor—self-assured, businesslike, unbowed by derogatory characterizations, without a trace of contrition, proud of its people and history, and ever-focused on the unrequited theft of Iran's popular sovereignty by a fascist theocracy.

Author and New York Times correspondent Stephen Kinzer, in his book on the 1953 CIA coup against nationalist Prime Minister Mohammed Mossadeq,[50] described the shared roots of Iranians' national character as a fusion of *"the continuing and often frustrating effort to find a synthesis between Islam ... and the rich heritage of pre-Islamic times"*; *"the thirst for just leadership, of which they have enjoyed precious little"*; and *"a tragic view of life rooted in a sense of martyrdom and communal pain."* While Mr. Kinzer is no MEK supporter and made this observation about the Iranian people as a whole, outsiders will recognize each of these characteristics in MEK members. For all the unusual aspects of their lives as regime opponents and exiled dissidents, the *Mojahedin* are, above all, Iranians.

Reviled for so long, the MEK's members and supporters will continue to endure unflattering descriptions that utterly fail to grasp their central motivation and source of self-respect. Those who make the effort to better understand the MEK will find a community of survivors whose collective quest is based not on keeping dark secrets but on exposing the past—a quietly proud society of educated and capable men and women bound not by cult-like dependency but by unity of purpose in the face of unspeakable loss and adversity. Accused of disloyalty to their homeland, they are sustained by the conviction that they have sacrificed more than any to help deliver long-deferred justice and self-determination to the nation.

Professor Abrahamian, perhaps anticipating that the MEK's essential character might not emerge through his scholarly recounting of details on the group's history, prefaced his study of the MEK with a quote from Naser Sadeq, a senior MEK member arrested and sent before the Shah's military tribunal in 1972. Addressing the judges before his sentence was pronounced, Naser Sadeq said this:

> "You have tortured us, convicted us in your kangaroo courts, and now you are about to sign our death warrants. Have you ever stopped to think why so many young intellectuals like us are willing to join the armed struggle, spend their whole lives in prison, and if necessary shed their blood? Have you ever asked yourself why so many of us are willing to make the supreme sacrifice?"

NOTES

1. See United States Court of Appeals for the District of Columbia Circuit, No. 09-1059, Decided July 16, 2010, p. 16.
2. US Department of Defense, "Maj. Gen. Odierno Videoteleconference from Baghdad," June 18, 2003, see http://www.defense.gov/transcripts/transcript.aspx?transcriptid=2757. Here is the full exchange:
Q: General, this is Nathan Hodge again, from Defense Week. Quick question about the Mujahideen-e Khalq, the People's Mujahideen: Have they been fully disarmed? And if not, have they been allowed to hold on to any small arms? And what kind of materiel and weapons, heavy equipment, did you confiscate from them?
Odierno: They have been completely disarmed. We have taken all small arms and all heavy equipment. They had about 10,000 small arms, and they had about 2,200 pieces of equipment, to include about 300 tanks, about 250 armored personnel carriers and about 250 artillery pieces. And we disarmed all of that equipment from them about 30 days ago.
3. "The United Nations helps to break Iranian dissidents," *Tribune de Geneve,* August 31, 2012.
4. The author's December 7, 2011 testimony before the House Committee on Foreign Affairs Subcommittee on Oversight and Investigations and Subcommittee on the Middle East and South Asia, as well as the author's August 16, 2011 assessment entitled, "Mujahedin-e Khalq (MEK/PMOI) and the Search for Ground Truth About its Activities and Nature" are posted as a single document on the House of Representatives website. See http://archives.republicans.foreignaffairs.house.gov/112/blo120711.pdf.
5. Office of the Spokesperson, U.S. Department of State, "Coordinator for Counterterrorism Daniel Benjamin and Special Advisor to the Secretary on Camp Ashraf Ambassador Daniel Fried on the Mujahedin-e Khalq (MEK) Designation and the Current Situation at Camp Ashraf," via teleconference, July 6, 2012.
6. CBC Radio-Canada, "Mujahideen-e-Khalq," August 17, 2011.
7. Blanchfield, Mike, "Judge criticizes CSIS, Crown over seige trial; Only two of 21 Iranian Embassy protesters jailed," *Ottawa Citizen,* September 10, 1994, p. C1.
8. MEK sources say Massoud Rajavi never went to the US embassy site during the hostage crisis, one reason being that his personal security could not have been assured in the presence of armed elements loyal to Ayatollah Khomeini.
9. Abrahamian, Ervand, *The Iranian Mojahedin* (New Haven: Yale University Press, 2009).
10. Boroujerdi, Mehrzad, *Iranian Intellectuals and the West: The Tormented Triumph of Nativism* (Syracuse: Syracuse University Press, 1996), pp. 117-119.
11. "We are on the Offensive," *Time,* September 14, 1981.
12. Ball, George W., "Iran's Bleak Future," *The Washington Post,* August 19, 1981.

13. The Tehran daily *Ettela'at*, on May 30, 1990, quoted Mohammed Yazdi, who became Chief Justice of Iran in 1989, referring to *"the Imam's hand-written judicial order"* in 1980 condemning *"the totality of the [MEK] organization and its infrastructure … so that there would be no hesitation in terming activities by these individuals as waging war on God …."*
14. *Daily Hansard*, March 27, 2001, Column 176, http://www.publications.parliament.uk/pa/ld200001/ldhansrd/vo010327/text/10327-16.htm.
15. Bakhash, Shaul, *The Reign of the Ayatollahs* (New York, Basic Books, 1984), p. 123.
16. This charge had some justification. See the author's August 2011 assessment, Op. cit., second page of Introduction, in which a senior US policy official acknowledged that designating the MEK as a terrorist group had been a "goodwill gesture" to Tehran.
17. See http://www.state.gov/j/ct/rls/other/des/123085.htm.
18. Goulka, Jeremiah, Hansell, Lydia, Wilke, Elizabeth, and Larson, Judith, *The Mujahedin-e Khalq in Iraq—A Policy Conundrum* (Washington DC, RAND National Defense Research Institute, 2009), www.rand.org/pubs/monographs/MG871.html.
19. *The Department of Defense Dictionary of Military and Associated Terms, 8 November 2010 (As Amended Through 15 December 2012)*, p. A38, lists the acronym "CULT" but this refers to "common-user land transportation."
20. See Goulka, Jeremiah, "The Cult of MEK," *The American Prospect*, July 18, 2012.
21. "Former UN human rights chief in Baghdad Tahar Boumedra: Why I Quit the UN in Iraq," *The Hill* Global Affairs Blog, August 22, 2012, see http://thehill.com/blogs/global-affairs/guest-commentary/244733-former-un-human-rights-chief-in-baghdad-tahar-boumedra-why-i-quit-the-un-in-iraq. See also http://archives.republicans.foreignaffairs.house.gov/112/75862.pdf and http://www.youtube.com/watch?v=rdKl7aOodRA.
22. USCA Case #12-1118, Document #1374468, letter dated May 14, 2012 from Deputy Assistant Attorney General Beth S. Brinkman to Andrew L. Frey, Esquire, counsel to People's Mojahedin Organization of Iran.
23. *No Exit - Human Rights Abuses Inside the Mojahedin Khalq Camps*, Human Rights Watch, May 2005, http://www.hrw.org/reports/2005/05/18/no-exit.
24. An AFP story on January 2, 2013 reported the public release by the NCRI of a 'draft' UNHCR memorandum titled "Temporary Transit Location for ex-Ashraf residents in Camp Liberty," dated January 19, 2012; the released UN document says, "From the technical point of view, UNHCR cannot … certify that the above location [Camp Liberty] meets Humanitarian Standards according to the many existing standard books, i.e. UNHCR Handbook, SPHERE, WHO and others …." The story reinforced allegations made before Congress in September 2012 by ex-UN official Tahar Boumedra that the head of the UN mission in Iraq had suppressed information regarding the suitability of Camp Liberty to host over 3,000 Iranian exiles. See "Irak: le camp Liberty ne répond pas aux normes de l'ONU (opposition iranienne)," AFP, January 2, 2013.
25. U.S. Department of State, daily press briefing, July 26, 2004, http://2001-2009.state.gov/r/pa/prs/dpb/2004/34680.htm.
26. *Iran's Ministry of Intelligence and Security: A Profile*, A Report Prepared by the Federal Research Division, Library of Congress under an Interagency Agreement with the Combating Terrorism Technical Support Office's Irregular Warfare Support Program, December 2012, p. 26.
27. "Human Rights Watch's Report on the Mujahedin E-Khalq," *Congressional Record—Extensions of Remarks*, Vol. 151, No. 83, June 21, 2005, p. E1299, http://www.gpo.gov/fdsys/pkg/CREC-2005-06-21/html/CREC-2005-06-21-pt1-PgE1299.htm.
28. Letter from ICRC to Ministry of Foreign Affairs, Baghdad, September 16, 1992.
29. The author quotes here from two pamphlets published by the NCRI in France: *Women—A Force for Change*, consisting of excerpted lectures and speeches by Maryam Rajavi, issued in April 2010; and *Islamic Fundamentalism and the Question of Women*, containing a reprinted speech by Maryam Rajavi to an audience of women in March 2004.

30. Robertson, Geoffrey QC, *The Massacre of Political Prisoners in Iran, 1988* (Washington, DC: Abdorraham Bouramand Foundation, 2009). This independent foundation receives support from the National Endowment for Democracy among other sources.
31. See, for example, Lamb, Christina, "Khomeini fatwa 'led to killing of 30,000 in Iran,'" *The Sunday Telegraph* (UK), February 4, 2001.
32. Amnesty International, *Document—Iran: Violations of Human Rights 1987-1990,* December 1, 1990, p. 9. http://www.amnesty.org/en/library/asset/MDE13/021/1990/en/5c32759d-ee5e-11dd-9381-bdd29f83d3a8/mde130211990en.html.
33. "Background on the Mujahedin," forwarded under Memorandum from W. Tapley Bennet, Jr. Assistant Secretary of State for Legislative Affairs, to Rep. Lee Hamilton, Chairman, Subcommittee on Europe and the Middle East, Committee on Foreign Affairs, US House of Representatives, December 14, 1984. Note that this memo also described the divisions within the MEK that culminated when "a dedicated Marxist faction … broke away in 1975 and murdered several Mujahedin leaders who preferred to emphasize the Islamic content, as opposed to the Marxist orientation, of the organization …." As noted, the 2005 *Country Reports* attributed the killing of American advisors in Iran to this breakaway Marxist faction, and contemporaneous media reporting confirmed it as well.
34. Gordon, Michael, Schmitt, Eric, and Arango, Tim, "Flow of Arms to Syria Through Iraq Persists, to US Dismay," *New York Times,* December 1, 2012, http://www.nytimes.com/2012/12/02/world/middleeast/us-is-stumbling-in-effort-to-cut-syria-arms-flow.html?pagewanted=all.
35. Black, Ian, "Iran Confirms it has Forces in Syria and will take Military Action if Pushed," *The Guardian,* September 16, 2012, http://www.guardian.co.uk/world/2012/sep/16/iran-middleeast.
36. Chivers, C.J. "A Trail of Bullet Casings Leads from Africa's Wars to Back Iran," *New York Times,* January 11, 2013, p. A1, http://www.nytimes.com/2013/01/12/world/africa/a-trail-of-bullet-casings-leads-from-africas-wars-to-iran.html?pagewanted=all&_r=0.
37. Bronner, Ethan, "With Longer Reach, Rockets Bolster Hamas Arsenal," *New York Times,* November 17, 2012, http://www.nytimes.com/2012/11/18/world/middleeast/arms-with-long-reach-bolster-hamas.html.
38. See Shanker, Thom and Worth, Robert, "Yemen Seizes Sailboat Filled with Weapons, and U.S. Points to Iran," *New York Times,* January 28, 2013, http://www.nytimes.com/2013/01/29/world/middleeast/29military.html; and Worth, Robert F., "Seized Chinese Weapons Raise Concerns on Iran," *New York Times,* March 3, 2013, p. A14, http://www.nytimes.com/2013/03/03/world/middleeast/seized-arms-off-yemen-raise-alarm-over-iran.html?pagewanted=all.
39. Erdbrink, Thomas, "Film to Present Iran's View of 'Argo' Events," *New York Times,* January 11, 2013, p. A8, http://www.nytimes.com/2013/01/11/world/middleeast/as-academy-snubs-affleck-for-argo-iran-plans-own-movie.html?_r=0.
40. Iran's Defense Minister, General Ahmad Vahidi, is reportedly a suspect in having organized the worst terrorist attack in Argentina's history, the July 18, 1994 bombing of the Israel-Argentina Mutual Association (Jewish community center) in Buenos Aires, which killed 85 and injured over 250 others. See Bosoer, Fabian and Finchelstein, Federico, "Argentina's About-Face on Terror," *New York Times,* March 1, 2013, op-ed, http://www.nytimes.com/2013/03/02/opinion/why-is-argentinas-president-cozying-up-to-iran.html. The US District Court for the Southern District of New York, investigating claims of official Iranian involvement in the September 11, 2001 attacks in the US by *Al Qaeda,* cited the fact that *"Argentine investigators [had] determined that the decision to bomb the AMIA center was taken at the highest levels of Iran's government, which directed … Hizballah to perform the operation. Specifically, this direction was made by Iran's Supreme Leader Khamenei, President Rafsanjani, Foreign Minister Velayati, and MOIS Minister Fallahian—the 'Omar-e Vijeh' (or Special Matters Committee)—during an August 14, 1993 meeting in Mashad, Iran, also attended by [IRGC Commander] Mohzen Rezai, Ahmad Vahidi, Mohsen Rabbani, and Ahmad Reza Ashari."* See Case 1:03-cv-09848-GBD Document 294, filed December

22, 2011, "Findings of Fact and Conclusions of Law," para 96, http://information.iran911case.com/Havlish_Findings_of_Fact_and_Conclusions_of_Law_Signed_12-22-11.pdf; the court also found, with respect to the September 11, 2001 Al Qaeda attacks against the United States (para 118), that "There were two separate, but related ways in which Iran furnished material and direct support for the 9/11 terrorists' specific terrorist travel operation …." The Iranian government has, within the past 1-2 years, been accused of a role in terrorist attacks or foiled attacks in Kenya, Thailand, India, Georgia and Bulgaria.

41. Federal Research Division, Library of Congress, *Op. cit.*, p. 27.
42. The author has previously described Iran's effort, with the Iraqi government's cooperation, to control the fate of about 200 MEK 'leaders' among the larger population still detained inside Camp Liberty in Iraq. See "Former U.S. special envoy Lincoln P. Bloomfield, Jr.: Clinton made the right move delisting the MEK," *The Hill* (online), September 22, 2012, http://thehill.com/blogs/global-affairs/guest-commentary/263247-former-us-special-envoy-lincoln-p-bloomfield-jr-clinton-made-the-right-move-delisting-the-mek.
43. Stevenson, Struan MEP, "Iraq – A Basket Case Democracy!," *Huff Post Politics United Kingdom*, February 9, 2013, http://www.huffingtonpost.co.uk/struan-stevenson-mep/iraq-a-basket-case-democr_b_2651872.html.
44. "Shiite Militant Threatens Iranian Exiles In Iraq," Associated Press, February 26, 2013, http://www.npr.org/templates/story/story.php?storyId=172957236.
45. The MEK also denies fighting along with Saddam Hussein's forces against Iraq's northern Kurdish and southern Shi'ite populations when these areas revolted against the Baghdad regime in the spring of 1991; the State Department has always used the caveat "reportedly" in repeating these allegations, and no hard evidence has surfaced in the almost ten years since the Saddam Hussein regime's files were seized during Operation Iraqi Freedom (see author's August 2011 independent assessment, note 4 above). See also Cowell, Alan, "Ashraf Journal: Facing Iran, an Army with Resolve and Day Care," *New York Times*, June 5, 1991, in which the *Times* journalist visiting Camp Ashraf hears mention of only two National Liberation Army (MEK) operations during March and April 1991, a time when MEK forces are alleged to have supported Iraqi elite units and engaged in massacres of Iraqi Kurds and Shi'ites. The two operations mentioned in the article were against Iranian Revolutionary Guards crossing into Iraq "*apparently in an effort to take advantage of the chaos in Iraq ….*"
46. "Iran Executed 670 in 2011, says U.N. Investigator," *Reuters*, March 23, 2012.
47. See for example, comments of Iran's Deputy Intelligence Minister in *Iran Daily*, January 28, 2010, and similar press stories: the daily *Kayhan*, May 1, 2010; *Khabar Online*, June 13, 2010; *AFP*, May 15, 2010; and *Resalat*, November 15, 2010, of which the author has seen translations.
48. Engel, Richard, and Windrem, Robert, "Israel teams with terror group to kill Iran's nuclear scientists, U.S. officials tell NBC News," February 9, 2012, see http://rockcenter.nbcnews.com/_news/2012/02/09/10354553-israel-teams-with-terror-group-to-kill-irans-nuclear-scientists-us-officials-tell-nbc-news?lite.
49. According to Amnesty International, Gholamreza Khosravi Savadjani, arrested in 2008 and held in solitary confinement in several detention centers including Evin Prison for having allegedly supported IRANNTV, was given a death sentence in April 2012. International pressure, including by the Department of State and EU's Foreign Policy Chief Catherine Ashton, have resulted in a delay in carrying out of the verdict. See http://www.amnesty.org/en/news/iran-executions-2012-09-07; see also http://www.iranhumanrights.org/2012/09/khosravi/.
50. Kinzer, Stephen, *All the Shah's Men: An American Coup and the Roots of Middle East Terror* (Hoboken, NJ: John Wiley & Sons, Inc., 2003).

ABOUT THE AUTHOR

Lincoln P. Bloomfield, Jr. is a former U.S. Government official who most recently served as the U.S. Special Envoy for MANPADS Threat Reduction from 2008–09 (reducing the availability of shoulder-fired missiles to terrorist groups who could threaten aviation safety). Ambassador Bloomfield was U.S. Assistant Secretary of State for Political Military Affairs as well as Special Representative of the President and Secretary of State for Humanitarian Mine Action from 2001–2005. He previously served as Deputy Assistant Secretary of State for Near Eastern Affairs (1992–93), Deputy Assistant to the Vice President for National Security Affairs (1991–02), Member, U.S. Delegation to Philippine Bases Negotiations (1990-91), Member, U.S. Water Mediation in the Middle East (1989–90), and Principal Deputy Assistant Secretary of Defense for International Security Affairs (1988–89), among other policy positions in the Department of Defense (OSD/ISA) beginning in 1981.

He is a graduate of Harvard College (a.b. *cum laude*, Government, 1974) and the Fletcher School of Law and Diplomacy (M.A.L.D., 1980), where he was director of *The Fletcher Forum*, the school's foreign affairs journal.

Since 2008 Ambassador Bloomfield has served as Chairman of the Stimson Center in Washington, DC, a non-partisan security think tank. In addition, Mr. Bloomfield is President of Palmer Coates LLC, Operating Partner at Pegasus Capital Advisors L.P., Senior Advisor at ZeroBase Energy LLC and non-attorney Consultant to Akin Gump Strauss Hauer & Feld LLP. It was in this latter capacity that Mr. Bloomfield examined the issues in this study, beginning in early 2011.